Dhati is an incredible leader endowed with seasoned wisdom, prophetic urgency, and the gracious disposition that comes from a firsthand experience in the gospel. I have greatly benefited from his wisdom on this issue and through this book, you will also. *Advocates* is both touching and practical, prophetic and pastoral. Dhati has a way of nailing down the pivotal issues and painting a positive vision of the future. I am excited to recommend both him and *Advocates* to you!

J.D. Greear, PhD
62nd President, The Southern Baptist Convention
Pastor, The Summit Church, Raleigh-Durham, NC
Author, *Above All*

I met Dhati over a decade ago on a church planter's retreat. I knew then that he was a leader of leaders. Through his book—which he is actually living out pastor of a multiethnic, reconciled local church—he is leading us to a holistic vision of a reconciled church. Be prepared to learn afresh. I highly recommend this important book.

Derwin Gray
Founding and Lead Pastor, Transformation Church,
Indian Land, SC
Author, *The High Definition Leader*; *Limitless Life*

I am grateful to Dhati who, as a friend and brother in Christ, has never run away from the tension that comes from pursuing racial reconciliation. I believe, as he does, that the church's mission of evangelism and disciple-making will be hindered if we do not confront our divisions and pursue unity. Dhati is an incredible leader and his book approaches the subject from a clear, biblical foundation that encourages and equips believers to pursue unity in the midst of diversity.

Kevin Ezell
President, North American Mission Board

I've been to the neighborhood in Atlanta where Dhati not only leads a church, but where his family is entrenched as advocates of the gospel. I've read every word of this book and can tell it comes from his heart as a student of Scripture and a pastor of his community. All throughout I could detect Dhati's careful concern for what the text of Scripture has to say about reconciliation and how members of the local church can be obedient and practical in their own contexts. *Advocates* will give you a better imagination for how the gospel truly makes a difference when thinking about reconciliation, and for how Christians truly make a difference when acting with conviction.

Daniel Yang
Director, Send Institute

In matters of race and reconciliation, we've too often and too quickly taken the posture of aggravators, justifying that fighting is the biblical and righteous thing to do. After all, wasn't Dietrich Bonhoeffer the one that said, "Silence in the face of evil is itself evil"? In this book, Dhati masterfully explains the difference between being an aggravator and an advocate, and how we ought to respond as individuals and as the church in this age fraught with division. Don't miss this!

Daniel Im
Director of Church Multiplication for
NewChurches.com at LifeWay Christian Resources
Author, *No Silver Bullets*

We need a book like this right now. Fresh, winsome, and helpful, this book is full of insights into a topic that has divided so many of us over the years. Dhati's wisdom, pastoral heart, and biblical insight forged out of decades of experience make this a highly usable and accessible resource. This book will challenge you, enlighten you, convict you, and give you new tools, patterns, and practices on the long road to racial justice.

Michael "Stew" Stewart
Founding Director, Verge Network

ADVOCATES

ADVOCATES

THE NARROW PATH TO
RACIAL RECONCILIATION

DHATI LEWIS

PUBLISHING
NASHVILLE, TENNESSEE

978-1-5359-3467-1

Published by B&H Publishing Group
Nashville, Tennessee

Dewey Decimal Classification: 227.86
Subject Heading: PROBLEM SOLVING / BIBLE. N.T.
PHILEMON / CONFLICT MANAGEMENT

Cover design and illustration by Edward
Patton. Author photo © Chad Pritchard.

1 2 3 4 5 6 7 • 23 22 21 20 19

To my wife, Angela, who helped a struggling, insecure
young man find his identity in Christ.
And to Jesus, my Advocate, who makes reconciliation possible.

Acknowledgments

In my life and ministry, I have learned the incredible value of working with a team. The content of this book, the production of this book, and all the other things that go into a project like this would not be possible without the amazing team God has given me.

Angela, if you hadn't helped me find my identity in Christ, I would not be able to present this content from a biblical perspective. At a time in my life where the adjectives in front of "Christianity" defined me more than being in Christ, you showed me what it looks like to find security in Christ. You know who you are, and you don't change depending on what environment you are in. The security of your identity in Christ helped me see and learn how to place my own identity in him too. God has used you more than anyone else in my life to continually remind me who I am in Christ and who I am called to be. This is a gift I will be forever grateful for.

I would also like to thank Jessica for all the work you do—seen and unseen—to keep my life organized and keep me out of trouble. You are a faithful steward, always multiplying the resources we are given and helping our team thrive. Stephanie, thank you for not only editing content but for being a person I can genuinely think through these principles with and have conversations with that help lead us toward more holistic thinking. Kevin, I am so thankful for you entrusting me with the opportunity to lead the Send Network and am so excited to see what God does in the years ahead. Carlos, thank you for being such an encouragement to me, always coming alongside me and cheering me on.

To the Send Network and the many practitioners across the country who are genuinely wrestling with these issues, thank you. Most of you do not have stages or platforms, but you're genuinely wrestling through hard issues in your daily life in some of the most dense and diverse cities in North America. Thank you for allowing me to lead the network and for your faithfulness in pursuing God's heart for people to be reconciled.

And finally, I would like to thank my Blueprint family for being a healthy place where we can run to the tension together and people can have honest, difficult conversations that lead to authentic life change. And to the Blueprint elders and Titus 2 Women who co-labor together, thank you for your tireless work to help our family live out our theology as we navigate through hard and difficult seasons of family life.

Contents

Part 4: What Fears or Obstacles Will We Face? 105

Preface

My name is Dhati Lewis. I am a Black man, married to a White woman, pastoring a diverse church.

For about a decade, we have been learning and growing from the blessings and challenges we've faced as a diverse church. Having different people from different walks of life in the same church family is beautiful, but it's not easy.

Diversity is such a buzzword these days, and as pastors, we all seem to want it. It seems most Christians also want to be part of a diverse church. But I've found that once you are in one, you discover how much it challenges some of your most deeply imbedded theological convictions. Almost like you can be an expert in knowing your Bible, but when it comes to issues of race and division, the Bible can be forgotten or dismissed.

I've learned to be creative when it comes to showing our church family the ways division impacts us and the ways the gospel calls us toward authentic unity (not just the idea of unity). One Sunday morning, during one of our "race talks," I asked people to move to different sides of the room based on different labels the world uses to divide us. Whites and minorities had to stand on opposite sides of the room. Then Democrats and Republicans. We did this exercise several times, with the goal of having people see and feel and experience a real representation of the divisions that will keep happening if we don't proactively work toward unity. Afterward, we went to the Scriptures to find out if the Bible really has anything to say about these divisions.

The racial divisions in our nation and in our church have forced me over the last few years to look over and over again at Galatians, Romans, and Ephesians. I've studied these New Testament letters for years as a theology student, knowing how rich and robust they are. But I've recently studied them with a new perspective, because I recognized that each one directly addresses issues of division among racial groups. It is this re-discovery of the Bible's rich content addressing racial divides, along with my experiences pastoring my local church, that have given me a deep desire to want to give other believers and local churches handlebars to engage divisive issues of race.

Regardless of whether you're a veteran when it comes to engaging racial divisions, or if you're new to the table, this book is for you. The focus and thread throughout will be addressing the posture of our hearts in the ways we engage with personal, relational, and systemic issues of racial division. And no matter how saturated or new you are to racial division, aligning and re-aligning your heart toward Christ isn't something you graduate from. Have you ever been in a season where you felt like you needed more than the gospel? I know from my own experience that there have been times where I've thought, *Yeah, yeah, I get that Jesus died and rose again. But that's just the basic stuff. I want more than that.* And then as I look for "more," time and time again God brings me right back to the gospel.

The gospel message isn't something we graduate from. We don't move on to bigger and better things. The gospel *is* the bigger and better thing. Paul writes in Colossians 2:6, "So then, just as you have received Christ Jesus as Lord, continue to live in him . . ." The English Standard Version says it like this: "Therefore, as you received Christ Jesus the Lord, so walk in him." We come to Christ through the gospel. And we walk with Christ through the gospel.

This is the same concept I have applied to our heart's posture when it comes to dealing with matters of racial division. Ensuring that our heart is aligned with Christ is not a one-time item on a to-do list that we check off and move forward from; it's an ongoing work to fight to keep our heart in line with Christ. And that is why, regardless of your experience with this subject matter, my hope and prayer is that this book challenges and encourages you toward deeper and ongoing alignment with the heart of Christ.

Before we jump in, I want to stop and give you a few definitions and disclaimers. Please don't skip over this section to get to "the start of the book." Without this, we may not be on the same page when it comes to specific terms, and without defining our terms, we can't have a helpful conversation. In a day when so many arguments are shallow and tweetable, I want to have some space for nuance and reflection, and be able to press into the gray areas. So let's start by defining a few key terms.

Advocate

Webster's definition of an *advocate*:

1. one who pleads the cause of another; specifically: one who pleads the cause of another before a tribunal or judicial court

2. one who defends or maintains a cause or proposal

3. one who supports or promotes the interests of a cause or group[1]

How I will use the term *advocate*:

My use of the term throughout this book will align with the definitions above with the exception of one nuance. I make the distinction that *to be an advocate, you must have the goal of reconciliation*. Advocates advocate for reconciliation to Christ and to his body. If the goal of someone's "advocacy" is anything less than reconciliation, then, I would argue, it is not biblical advocacy.

Look at 1 John 2:1–2 where John writes, "My little children, I am writing you these things so that you may not sin. But if anyone does sin, we have an advocate with the Father—Jesus Christ the righteous one. He himself is the atoning sacrifice for our sins, and not only for ours, but also for those of the whole world." Jesus advocates for us and atones for our sins, making a way for us to be reconciled with him. The goal of biblical advocacy is reconciliation, and while we see it most clearly in Jesus, we also see it modeled by many others. In 1 Samuel 19, Jonathan advocates for David before his father (King Saul) in an effort to reconcile their relationship and spare David from being killed. In Acts 9:26–30, Barnabas advocates for Saul (Paul) when the disciples did not believe his conversion was authentic. In Galatians 2, Paul advocates for the Gentile believers when Peter refused to eat with them.

Being an advocate doesn't mean you have to engage in conflict perfectly, and it doesn't mean reconciliation always takes place. What's key here is the posture of your heart—your

---

[1] https://www.merriam-webster.com/dictionary/advocate

intentions. Everyone's going to make mistakes and misstep at times. The distinguishing mark of an advocate is a heart whose goal is reconciliation.

Aggravator

Webster's definition of an *aggravator*: one that aggravates[2]

1. to make worse, more serious, or more severe: to intensify unpleasantly
2. to rouse to displeasure or anger by usually persistent and often petty goading
3. to produce inflammation in[3]

How I will use the term *aggravator*:

My use of the term aggravator will be nuanced from the formal definition throughout the book. I will use the term aggravator to describe any type of engagement where the goal is *not* reconciliation. A person who engages issues or people without a heart set on reconciliation will only intensify division and produce greater inflammation that does not lead toward unity. You can think of it like throwing gasoline on the fires of division—aggravators only make it more severe.

There is a difference between an action that causes aggravation or irritation (in people or systems) and an action that is done with the heart posture of an aggravator. I know this is nuanced, but I think it's critical for us to understand.

Let's look at Jesus as an example. Remember when the religious leaders were misusing the temple and taking advantage of others? Look at Jesus' response. "Jesus went into the temple and

---

[2] https://www.merriam-webster.com/legal/aggravator
[3] https://www.merriam-webster.com/dictionary/aggravate

threw out all those buying and selling. He overturned the tables of the money changers and the chairs of those selling doves. He said to them, 'It is written, my house will be called a house of prayer, but you are making it a den of thieves!'" (Matt. 21:12–13). Did Jesus' response cause aggravation in the temple? Of course it did. But what was the posture of Jesus' heart? What was his motive? Reconciliation. The practices of the religious leaders were causing distraction and chaos that prevented people—specifically, Gentiles—from worshiping God, and therefore, prevented reconciliation between people and God. Jesus was working to stop sinful actions and unjust practices that were hindering people from truly knowing God, from being reconciled to him, and from being reconciled to one another.

So for the purposes of this book and this conversation, I am going to maintain a nuanced difference between advocates and aggravators that lies within the heart's motives. One who stirs up and disturbs the feelings of others or engages issues or people for any purpose other than reconciliation is an aggravator. Jesus is not an aggravator because Jesus' goal was always reconciliation.

Since the heart posture of reconciliation is the distinguishing factor between these two (advocates and aggravator), I also want to make sure you understand how I will use the word *reconciliation* throughout the book.

Reconciliation

Webster's definition of *reconciliation*:

1. to restore to friendship or harmony: to settle, resolve
2. to make consistent or congruous

3.   to cause to submit to or accept something
     unpleasant

4.   to check (a financial account) against
     another for accuracy[4]

The New Bible Dictionary's definition of *reconciliation*:

> Reconciliation properly applies not to good
> relations in general but to the doing away of an
> enmity, the bridging over of a quarrel. It implies
> that the parties being reconciled were formerly
> hostile to one another.[5]

The *Dictionary of Bible Themes*' definition of *reconciliation*:

> The restoration of fellowship between God
> and humanity and the resulting restoration of
> human relationships. The NT affirms that the
> reconciliation of the world to God is only pos-
> sible on the basis of the work of Jesus Christ.[6]

How I will use the term *reconciliation*:

Many Christians don't like the term reconciliation, especially
in regards to ethnic or racial issues, because in our common language, it seems to imply that there was a time when things were
not divided. "Restoring friendship" implies that there was once
a friendship to begin with. And, as many of us likely know, that
is not often our experience.[7] However, I think the biblical term

---

[4] https://www.merriam-webster.com/dictionary/reconciled

[5] D. R. Wood and Howard I. Marshall, *The New Bible Dictionary*, 3rd
ed. (Downers Grove, IL: InterVarsity Press, Logos, 1996).

[6] Martin H. Manser, *Dictionary of Bible Themes*, word 6716, Logos.

[7] This is especially true in the case of Black-White relations in the
United States.

goes back much further than our own limited experiences. We will explore this in more depth in a later chapter, but let's pause and take a quick look at 2 Corinthians 5:18–21:

> Everything is from God, who has reconciled us to himself through Christ and has given us the ministry of reconciliation. That is, in Christ, God was reconciling the world to himself, not counting their trespasses against them, and he has committed the message of reconciliation to us. Therefore, we are ambassadors for Christ, since God is making his appeal through us. We plead on Christ's behalf: "Be reconciled to God." He made the one who did not know sin to be sin for us, so that in him we might become the righteousness of God.

If reconciliation only means the restoration of a previous experience, then which of us would have hope of being reconciled to God? Before Christ we were enemies of God (Rom. 5:10), dead in our trespasses and sins (Col. 2:13), slaves to a different master (Rom. 6:20). In our lifetimes, all of us began as enemies of God. The reconciling work of the cross did not reconcile us back to our state as enemies—it went further, reconciling us back to God's original design for humanity and reconciling us forward toward the future hope of heaven. And that is the same type of reconciliation the gospel makes possible for us to have with one another! People have been divided by language, tribe, ethnicity, color, gender, age, wealth, and many more issues since the beginning of time. Praise God that is not what we are hoping to get back to! No, we want to be reconciled with one another, receiving one another into the favor that God originally designed and toward the promised peace coming to us when Jesus returns.

Because of the clarity with which the Scriptures use this term, I want to stick with it. If we have been given the "ministry of reconciliation," then I think it's worth taking the extra time to really press into what the word means in the Scriptures so that we can rightly apply it in our lives. And this leads us to my first disclaimer.

Disclaimer 1: I sometimes use ethnic reconciliation and racial reconciliation interchangeably.

While I know that the nuances between the words *ethnicity* and *race* can be very important in certain conversations, I am choosing to primarily use the terms *race* and *racial reconciliation*. I may use ethnic or ethnicity as a synonym at times but will primarily use race. I do believe that humans are all part of one race, the human race. We are not different species of humans. However, I've chosen to use race for two primary reasons. One, in everyday life and conversation, most people do not nuance between the terms *race* and *ethnicity*—and most (in my experience) tend to use the word race to describe divisions based on skin color, nationality, language, or tribe. Because *racial reconciliation* and *race* are more common terms in our North American context, I want to stick with them because they will communicate in a more effective way.

The second reason I've chosen to use these terms is based on the line of thought excellently described in Michael Emerson and Christian Smith's book, *Divided by Faith*. They argue that although race is a social construct (meaning society basically made it up, and there's no scientific support for its existence), because it has been socially constructed in America, then it is accurate and appropriate to use the term race in this context.[8]

So, to make sure we are *absolutely* clear, when I use the term racial reconciliation, I am referring to when people or people groups divided by tribe, language, skin color, or nationality, are restored through justice, mercy, and forgiveness, to God's original design for relationships with him and with one another.

Disclaimer 2: I am using a holistic understanding of biblical justice.

If you asked ten people to define *justice*, you would probably get ten different answers. And if you gave those same ten people a scenario of injustice, you would likely get ten different responses as to what it would look like for justice to take place. In his book *The Little Book of Biblical Justice*, Chris Marshall gives an excellent example about how you can have two adamant defenders of justice, but one will defend capital punishment as a "matter of just desserts," while another will argue adamantly that the punishment is unjust because it is an "affront to human dignity."[9] So even in circumstances where everyone agrees justice is needed, we staunchly maintain different ideas of what justice looks like. Our cultural backgrounds, religious views, and life experiences shape our views of justice.[10]

This is why, for the Christian, we must be careful to understand justice biblically, being mindful not to let our cultural

---

[8] Michael O. Emerson and Christian Smith, *Divided by Faith: Evangelical Religion and the Problem of Race in America* (New York: Oxford University Press, 2000), 8.

[9] Chris Marshall, *The Little Book of Biblical Justice* (Intercourse, PA: Good Books, 2005), 5, location 92, Kindle.

[10] Ibid., 7, location 130, Kindle.

biases cloud what God says is true about justice. Justice begins in the nature of God, himself.[11]

Justice plays a critical role in reconciliation, and as reconciliation is the focus of this book, I want to dedicate some space to explaining how I will use the term *justice* throughout. But please understand that much will be left unsaid about justice—much that is important to the work of reconciliation. I would encourage you to take time to explore it more on your own.

In his book, Marshall makes a compelling, biblical argument that justice is about relationships, not mere punishment.[12] Take a look at Isaiah 30:18, "'Therefore the LORD waits to be gracious to you; therefore he will rise up to show mercy to you. For the LORD is a God of justice; blessed are all those who wait for him' (Isa. 30:18, compare with Ps. 85:10)."[13]

The verse above clearly states that God will show mercy *because* he is a God of justice. The two are not in conflict. Mercy is part of God's justice. This could not be true if justice were primarily about punishment or equal treatment. Mercy can only be part of justice if justice is primarily about the restoration of relationships.[14] And since biblical justice is all about restoring relationships, it touches on every area of life (because all areas of life impact our relationships!).

The relational focus of justice also explains why biblical justice is simultaneously impartial and partial. Marshall clearly shows how in situations of criminal justice and determining guilt, biblical justice demands impartiality. Israelite or Gentile, rich or poor, man or woman—no category of person was to get

---

[11] Ibid., 22, location 319, Kindle.

[12] Ibid., 35, location 507, Kindle.

[13] Ibid., 38, location 543, Kindle.

[14] Ibid., 36, location 518, Kindle.

special treatment in determining guilt. However, when it comes to social justice, biblical justice demands partiality, paying special attention to the marginalized, the poor, the foreigner, and the outcast. God is not shy about ensuring that the law distributed power, wealth, and resources in such a way that would ensure the vulnerable were taken care of.[15] Just consider the following ways God provided for the marginalized through the Old Testament law:

> "When an alien resides with you in your land,
> you must not oppress him. You will regard the
> alien who resides with you as the native-born
> among you. You are to love him as yourself, for
> you were aliens in the land of Egypt; I am the
> LORD your God." (Lev. 19:33–34)

> "Do not return a slave to his master when he
> has escaped from his master to you. Let him live
> among you wherever he wants within your city
> gates. Do not mistreat him." (Deut. 23:15–16)

The prophets, God's covenant lawyers who called his people back to faithfulness, constantly spoke against their mistreatment of the poor, their failure to ensure justice for the marginalized:

> "Wash yourselves. Cleanse yourselves. Remove
> your evil deeds from my sight. Stop doing
> evil. Learn to do what is good. Pursue justice.
> Correct the oppressor. Defend the rights of
> the fatherless. Plead the widow's cause." (Isa.
> 1:16–17)

---

[15] Ibid., 38, location 553, Kindle.

> "This is what the LORD says: Administer
> justice and righteousness. Rescue the victim of
> robbery from his oppressor. Don't exploit or
> brutalize the resident alien, the fatherless, or
> the widow. Don't shed innocent blood in this
> place." (Jer. 22:3)

And just in case we are tempted to think this is just an Old Testament issue, James the brother of Jesus believed these matters were central to true Christianity: "Pure and undefiled religion before God the Father is this: to look after orphans and widows in their distress and to keep oneself unstained from the world" (James 1:27).

If biblical justice is all about the restoration of relationships, then those parameters should guide our views and the way we implement justice.

Now, just because punishment is not the aim of justice, does not mean that punishment doesn't have a place in biblical justice. Many times it is only *through* punishment that restoration and reconciliation can take place. When damage has been done, restoration needs to take place in different ways: "restoration of the victim to wholeness, restoration of the offender to right standing in the community, and restoration of the wider society to peace and freedom from fear, sin, and pollution."[16] Many times that type of holistic restoration does not come without punishment, without consequences for the injustice that damaged the relationships in the first place.[17]

Think about it in terms of parenting. No matter how wonderfully thought-out your boundaries are, your kids are going to

---

[16] Ibid., 44, location 638, Kindle.
[17] Ibid.

find a way to challenge them. Kids push boundaries. And when they cross a boundary, it is the responsibility of a parent to identify appropriate consequences. Why? So that relationship can be restored—because where boundaries are crossed or relationships are breached, it is often *through consequences* that repentance and restoration can take place. Consequences pave the way for the parent-child relationship (or child-child relationship, friendship, etc.) to be restored to a healthy place. This same principle applies to issues on a larger scale, also.

Of course, the greatest example of this is the gospel itself. The heart of the gospel is reconciliation—between humans and God, and between humans and one another. But there had to be punishment for God's merciful justice to be expressed; Jesus had to bear the punishment for our sins. When he did, he made a way for reconciliation and restoration.

I do not think you can have true reconciliation without justice. (Because how can relationships be reconciled if they have not been restored through justice?) But I think that we must shift our understanding of justice to align with biblical justice (and not cultural or Western ideals of justice) so that our understanding of reconciliation and how to engage people, issues, and systems across lines of division will also shift to be in line with biblical reconciliation.

Because of my background, education, experiences, and field of study, I am most equipped to write on the latter, so that is the focus of this work: how to engage people and systems of injustice with a heart posture that aligns with Christ. We will dive deep into the posture of our hearts, exploring thought patterns, and identifying key principles of engagement that apply to a variety of situations. I believe identity drives activity, so I want the focus of this work to be on embracing the identity of an advocate.

When we do this, we will be equipped to engage in holistic reconciliation (involving restoration and justice, both individually and systemically) in our communities from a heart posture that is in line with Christ.

I have not even scratched the surface of the conversation that needs to be had about holistic justice. But I did want to take time to ask you to consider a holistic understanding of justice, recognizing its critical part in reconciliation, so that you have clarity when I mention it throughout the book. There may be times when I expand more or other times when I mention it briefly. But know that I do not mention it lightly or mean to gloss over it as if there were not pages and pages that could be (and have been) written on the subject.

Disclaimer 3: If you're looking for me to take a political side, I won't.

Conversations and issues surrounding race, justice, and reconciliation often end up blending with political conversations and issues. And while I have political opinions, this book is not the place where I will be defending or explaining those. I also will not demean or belittle political views different from my own. I truly believe most of our political engagement is lacking in biblical basis, balanced perspective, and safe environments to discuss. So when I engage political issues throughout the book, my goal is to show ways to maintain a biblical basis and a balanced perspective, and how to create safe environments so that all parties involved can move toward reconciliation.

Of these three goals (maintaining biblical basis, keeping a balanced perspective, and creating safe environments), I think safe environments are most obviously missing from our churches. How do we create spaces where people can have different opinions under an umbrella of love and grace? Where the goal is not to change people's perspectives, but to allow everyone to show up so that we can be together and understand one another? When there is safety for you to fully express your views in a space where you feel heard and truly listened to, you will come to a place where you feel safe to allow your views to be challenged by others. But if we don't have spaces where views can be fully expressed, we won't ever have spaces where it is safe to challenge one another's views. So in the political issues that arise because of race, my goal in this book is to give handlebars for creating safe spaces for engagement while maintaining a heart that is aligned with Christ.

Disclaimer 4: I'm Black.

I'm Black, and my wife is White. I recognize that my heritage, story, marriage, and family history play a huge part in my perspectives. Throughout the book, I hope to share some of those things with you so you can better see how the Lord has forced me to wrestle with these issues and how they have impacted the way I think, lead, and pastor today.

Disclaimer 5: I don't believe you can be a healthy Christian apart from the local church.

I am writing this book as a follower of Christ and local church pastor writing to other followers of Christ in local churches. I do not believe we can live out principles of reconciliation with a lost world if we cannot apply those principles with one another, and I don't believe we can apply them with one another apart from the life of the local church. The natural conclusion of that is, if you aren't part of a local body of Christ, I don't believe you can live out the commands of Scripture.

How can we fulfill all of the "one anothers" if we have no one to be patient with, or kind to, or to love? We have to wrestle through problems with real people. The principles in this book just won't work without a community to live them with. I love what pastor and Civil Rights activist John M. Perkins said about this issue: "The big deal is we think the power is in us individually. The power is in us collectively. It is in the church."[18] Pastor and author Thabiti Anyabwile echoes this sentiment when he writes,

> We desperately need the church for love, for
> maturity and preparedness, for spiritual care.
> It is arrogant, rebellious, self-reliant, God-
> indicting pride to conclude that the church is
> an optional extra to the Christian life. We need
> everything God designs for us. Everything. To
> reject what God designs for His glory and our
> good is spiritual suicide. To reject the church is
> to take your own spiritual life.[19]

To combine what these two men said means that not only do we need the church for our personal good (growth, care, etc.), but we need the church in order to fully access and display the power of God. I wholeheartedly affirm this truth and am writing to you with this assumption undergirding everything I write.

---

[18] John M. Perkins quote retrieved December 7, 2018 from crcc.usc.edu website: https://crcc.usc.edu/Black-lives-matter-is-a-Black-church-matter/.

[19] *The Local Church* by Thabiti Anyabwile taken from *Don't Call It a Comeback*, edited by Kevin DeYoung (Wheaton, IL: Crossway, 2011), 211.

Where We're Headed

I hope these definitions and disclaimers were helpful to you. I really did feel like they were critical to the conversation I hope to start with you in the chapters ahead. I think it's only fair to give you a clear baseline understanding of who I am and where I'm writing from, because with all the different people writing on this subject today, it seems like these terms can take on a different meaning depending on where and how you use them.

My prayer for you as you turn the next page is that it would be the next step in your journey toward living out your identity as an advocate for Christ, that you would gain more tools for how to engage racial division in healthy, biblical ways, and that you would know Jesus better because of it.

PART 1

WHERE ARE WE?

CHAPTER 1

Awareness

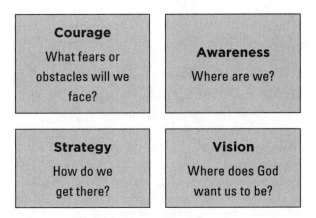

Courage	Awareness
What fears or obstacles will we face?	Where are we?

Strategy	Vision
How do we get there?	Where does God want us to be?

I'm often asked to coach church planters, pastors, and others on matters related to racial reconciliation in the church. It's a common talking point, and more and more, pastors are feeling the need to lead well in this regard. I use the same basic outline for those coaching sessions, asking and answering four questions: 1) Where are we? 2) Where does God want us to be? 3) How do we get there? 4) What fears or obstacles will keep us from getting there? These four questions will provide the structure for this book as we walk through awareness, vision, strategy, and courage.

Awareness: Where Are We?

It doesn't take much time scrolling through social media, watching the news, or reading the paper to see that our country is divided, and so are our churches. When I scroll through Twitter, I see Christians fighting for their own opinions and voices more than they are fighting to love one another. Facebook has become grounds for vilifying responses and patronizing remarks, none of which actually help bridge the divide. But social media is only reflecting what's going on in reality. If we are overrun with aggravators in the virtual world, then you'd better believe there is no shortage of aggravating going on in people's everyday lives. Sure, the form of aggravation might look different without the computer screen to hide behind, but the impact will remain. When I look at where we are, I think most of us, on most days, are aggravators.

This issue of racial division is close to my heart for a lot of different reasons. I wasn't raised in the church. I grew up around pro-Black politics with family members desiring to join the Black Panther party. And coming from that kind of background, I was hit hard with the realities of ethnic division when one day, as a young Christian, I realized I was falling in love with a White woman.

Now I was the guy on campus who was known as the "racial reconciliation guy." I was the one always asking, "Can't we all just get along?" I even started a ministry called B.A.S.I.C. (Brothers and Sisters in Christ) that focused on different races coming together. I really wanted racial unity, but truthfully, I only wanted it on a certain level. I only wanted it as long as it was external.

To be honest, when it came down to the deepest issues of my heart and my life, I was like, "Hold up, God. I don't know if I can marry a White woman." Because there I was, an African American man with a strong pro-Black family background, now immersed in predominantly White settings. Because of my theological convictions, I was a member of a White church and a staff member of Campus Crusade for Christ, a predominantly White organization. And even though my "branch" of the ministry (Impact) was geared toward African American students, I was still surrounded by White people in my daily life. And then, on top of that, I started falling in love with a White woman! It caused a major personal crisis—*did this mean I was an Uncle Tom? A sellout?*

You see, I had a preference for the way I wanted the church to look. I wanted to be a kind of community that you take a picture of and say, "Look how diverse we are!" But when it came down to the depths of my heart and the issues that really mattered, I knew I still had preferences. I even went so far as to tell Angie (my wife now) that she was the type of woman I'd like to marry if she were Black. And God had to painfully convict this part of my heart that only wanted superficial unity. And as he did, I not only fell in love with Angie, but I asked her to marry me, and she said yes.

Unfortunately, this isn't the happy ending for our story. I wasn't the only one who had a heart issue with the idea of an interracial marriage. We started our premarital counseling with a couple who were leaders in our church and the organization I worked for. They were both White and were well respected in our community. As soon as our session started, I sensed a strong tension in the room. So, being the observant person that I am, I decided to break the ice. "Okay. So I'm Black. And Angie's White. Let's just get that part out in the open."

While it initially caused a few laughs, things were only okay on the surface. Soon after we started our counseling, Angie and I had our first major disagreement. It wasn't anything unusual for couples to struggle with, but we needed help learning how to communicate through it. So we took our argument to our counselors, and as Angie shared her frustration, do you know what their response was? They gave her an article to read. And the article was about why people who marry interracially are trying to get back at their parents and why it is complete disobedience. This was their advice.

The sad reality is, I really believe they thought they were genuinely helping us.

This type of "counsel" wasn't limited to our White leaders. I talked to many of my African American brothers and sisters in Christ, and I asked them, "Would you rather me marry a Black non-Christian or a White Christian?" And more often than not, they said a Black non-Christian. And they would go through all their reasons and give me all kinds of justifications about how we are losing all of our Black men and this or that. And just like our counselors, they had all the best intentions in the world. The problem was that not one person was willing to call division sin. No one was willing to say racial discrimination is wrong.

So before we jump into the ins and outs of Advocates and Aggravators, I want to ask you a question. *Are you willing to call any division that is caused by racism, discrimination, or prejudice a spiritual and moral problem?* Are you willing to call it sin? Are we, together, willing to call it sin?

This is the framework that I am coming from. And if we don't start here together, the rest of this book won't resonate with your heart at all.

Racial Division in the Early Church

I want to take a brief detour to consider a story from the early church in Acts 6. In this short passage we get huge insights into what God thinks about racial division and how his church should respond. The text makes it clear that racial division is a real problem that demands real solutions that can lead to real transformation. Here's how the story begins:

> In those days, as the disciples were increasing in number, there arose a complaint by the Hellenistic Jews against the Hebraic Jews that their widows were being overlooked in the daily distribution. (Acts 6:1)

Did you catch that? *One racial group was being overlooked by another racial group in the daily distribution of food.* This was a real problem. The divisions of the world had crept into the church. And how did the church respond? Let's look.

> The Twelve summoned the whole company of the disciples and said, "It would not be right for us to give up preaching the word of God to wait on tables. Brothers and sisters, select from

among you seven men of good reputation, full
of the Spirit and wisdom, whom we can appoint
to this duty. But we will devote ourselves to
prayer and to the ministry of the word." This
proposal pleased the whole company. So they
chose Stephen, a man full of faith and the
Holy Spirit, and Philip, Prochorus, Nicanor,
Timon, Parmenas, and Nicolaus, a convert
from Antioch. They had them stand before the
apostles, who prayed and laid their hands on
them. (Acts 6:2–6)

The racial divisions were considered to be so grievous and
serious that for the first time in the whole book of Acts, the
entire church stops and gathers together. In this text, there's kind
of this sense of, "Look. The world is going to have its divisions.
But not in God's house. When the divisions of the world become
the divisions of the church, we have to stop everything and
address it. This cannot be." And so they stopped and gathered
everyone together.

Historically, we've used this passage to tell the story of how
we get deacons. While that may be the case, it's not the point
of the text—there is so much more going on in these verses.
We see how the church not only stops to gather, but how they
identify real solutions. They name seven Hellenistic (Greek,
Gentile) men who have authority and responsibility to oversee
restoration and justice in this issue. Their solution was specific
and culturally sensitive, as it took authority away from those who
were abusing it (the Hebraic Jews) and intentionally placed it with

seven Hellenistic Jews who could best address the issue at hand.[1] In other words, the members of the oppressed party (Gentiles) were given authority, rather than members of the oppressing party (Jews). And then, in the very next verses, we see that those real solutions led to real transformation:

> So the word of God spread, the disciples in
> Jerusalem increased greatly in number, and a
> large group of priests became obedient to the
> faith. (Acts 6:7)

Acts 6:7 is the second major benchmark in the book of Acts where a multitude of people come to know the Lord. (The first is in Acts 2:47.) But here we not only see a multitude come to faith, Luke also specifically mentions that a large group of priests became obedient to the faith. Why?

This racial division is a problem they've likely had for a while. So now they are looking at this new church and waiting to see how they will handle the division. And what they see is supernatural. The church's response communicates that they aren't willing to gloss over the problem, that they are willing to call racial division sin, and that they are willing to give real solutions to the division. The early church viewed it as their spiritual and moral obligation to address issues of racial division. And as the priests saw this, they had to recognize something was different about this community—and many of them became obedient to the faith.

Are we willing to do the same? If God has given us the ministry of reconciliation (2 Cor. 5:19), then we must recognize

---

[1] J. D. Barry and L. Wentz, eds., *The Lexham Bible Dictionary* (Bellingham, WA: Lexham Press, 2012), "Acts 6:1–6." Found at www.logos.com.

that when our heart's posture is divisive or when we stand idly by in the midst of division, we are in opposition to God's mission. Racial divisions aren't simply a social issue reserved for politicians or civic leaders to handle. This is a spiritual and moral problem.

One simple way we can get a glimpse into how racial divisions are manifesting in the church today is to look at polling percentages. Over 80 percent of Black Evangelicals voted for President Obama in 2008[2] while over 80 percent of White Evangelicals voted for President Trump in 2016.[3] Those stats alone reveal how Christians today are more aligned with their racial perspectives than we are united in Christ.

During the 2015 ERLC Leadership Summit, Kevin Smith commented, "Our lack of unity and oneness is a direct contradiction of our missiological goal: disciples of all nations."[4] These divisions within the church are negatively impacting our mission. The divisions of the world have crept into the church. So the question is, *does the church have real solutions for this division?*

Praise God, the answer is a resounding yes! Or, at the least, a qualified yes—the church *can* have real solutions for this division. But we have to start by being willing to call any division caused by racism, discrimination, or prejudice a spiritual and moral problem. We must be willing to call it sin.

Later on, we will talk more about the solutions. But let's stick to the awareness phase for now. So far, we've talked about

---

[2] http://www.pewforum.org/2012/11/07/how-the-faithful-voted-2012-preliminary-exit-poll-analysis/

[3] http://www.pewresearch.org/fact-tank/2016/11/09/how-the-faithful-voted-a-preliminary-2016-analysis/

[4] Kevin Smith, 2015 ERLC Leadership Summit, https://leadership.lifeway.com/2015/04/09/10-quotes-from-the-erlc-leadership-summit-on-race/.

recognizing the state of division that exists in our nation and our churches, we've talked about being willing to call division sin, and now I want to take a deeper look into what it means to be an aggravator.

Three Kinds of Aggravators

I really believe that most of us live a lot of our lives as aggravators. And if we aren't aware of how this can manifest, then we won't fully be able to engage as advocates. Being aware is a critical first step.

So I want to break it down and look at three different types of aggravators. I'm going to use the fight, flight, and freeze responses as the framework for the different types of aggravators. These reactions are proven to be our typical responses to threats of danger or fear.[5] They are survival mechanisms that your body chemically supports with hormones and nervous system responses in order to ensure your survival.[6]

So, think about a situation with a bully. There are some of us who, when faced with a bully at school, wouldn't think twice about fighting back. We think that the best way to escape the danger would be to simply fight it until it goes away. Others may have an intuitive response to run from the danger, so they run inside and stay off the playground. Still others believe that the best way to survive a bully is if the bully doesn't notice you, so they freeze, they hide, they do all they can to remain invisible to the bully. Each of these three responses are efforts to survive.

---

[5] https://www.psychologytoday.com/us/blog/evolution-the-self/201507/trauma-and-the-freeze-response-good-bad-or-both

[6] Ibid.

And surviving is good! God wired our brains to have these very normal responses to danger. But think about this in terms of the military. Those in the armed forces are trained to respond differently from their instincts in order to take risks, achieve a common goal, and complete their mission. And the same is true for us. It's not that our instincts are bad, but like soldiers, we must be trained so that our responses align with the heart and direction of our Commanding Officer.

Any of these responses can be easily triggered in us. Sure, they're most obvious if we are being chased by an angry dog or get in a fistfight. But there are other types of dangers and fears that can trigger these same responses. The fear of rejection, disapproval, vulnerability, no longer being connected with a group, losing reputation, being misunderstood, saying the wrong thing, not being heard—the list could go on and on. And when we are faced with these fears and dangers, our initial response is most often fight, flight, or freeze. But when paired with a heart that isn't seeking reconciliation, these responses are characteristic of an aggravator who is not seeking reconciliation—only self-interest or survival.

We are going to take a deep dive and consider how each of these responses can be aggravating and cause further divisions.

A Fighting Aggravator

Using the baseline understanding of the fight, flight, freeze responses, we see that each response is triggered by a perceived danger. So what danger or perceived danger triggers the fight response in a fighting aggravator?

Perceived Danger

In regard to issues of racial division, this trigger often depends on what your race is. For a racial minority, one threat is any kind of attempt to simply maintain the status quo. Living within a system set up to keep minorities at a disadvantage[7] poses a serious threat to the success and well-being of minorities, keeping them marginalized and disenfranchised.[8] In the face of this threat, many aggravators begin to fight.

For those in the racial majority, one perceived danger that triggers the fight response could be a response to accusations of being racist or privileged, or even a fear of change in the status quo. Those in majority culture have the advantage of not feeling the negative effects of the status quo. Many are aware of their privilege, so the prospect of the scales tilting (to make things level again) may seem to them like the scales are actually going to tilt to their disadvantage.

This daunting fear of change and the unknown can be enough to trigger a powerful response. All you have to do to see this is scroll through your social media. Many fighting aggravators in the majority culture will lash out or fly off the handle in response to even a hint at the possibility that they might be in some way privileged, and that something might need to change to help those at a disadvantage. If you feel the urge to lash out whenever conversations about race arise, you may be a fighting aggravator.

STRENGTHS AND WEAKNESSES

Each type of aggravator, while ultimately falling short of being an advocate, does have certain strengths. Some fighting

---

[7] For more on this, see *Divided by Faith* by Emerson and Smith; *White Awake* by Daniel Hill; *Many Colors* by Soong-Chan Rah (see chapter 6); *The Next Evangelicalism* by Soong-Chan Rah (see chapter 3); https://www.paul tripp.com/articles/posts/my-confession-toward-a-more-balanced-gospel.

[8] Emerson and Smith, *Divided by Faith*, 9, 45, 48.

aggravators, for example, tend to be excellent truth tellers. They see the lines of right and wrong very distinctly and are not afraid to call people toward justice. In many ways, this type of aggravator has a prophetic voice in our day. They are willing to take action quickly and make personal sacrifices for their cause. Their passion creates an open dialogue of genuine fear, hurt, and anger. This is a great strength because, with the other types of aggravators, you tend to have to go deep-sea diving to figure out what they are really feeling.

On the flip side of this, most fighting aggravators struggle with seeing or telling the whole story. They focus in on one truth (whether that be a truth of their emotion or a truth of the situation) and neglect to consider how all the other parts of the story combine to create a holistic picture. They leave out parts of the story that contradict the point they want to make and often highlight specific aspects of the situation that, isolated from the whole story, incite fear in those they want to persuade.

Another weakness of the fighting aggravator comes in their motto to "keep it real." The problem is that many times keeping it real means keeping it mean and insensitive—and there is nothing innately prophetic about speaking harsh words. Too often we identify more with what our flesh says is true than what God says is true, and this results in a "keeping it real" that aligns with our emotions and fleshly thoughts rather than with God's agenda for reconciliation. One danger for a fighting aggravator is to view themselves as prophets when they are only self-appointed prophets, speaking only from their viewpoint. They miss an opportunity to use their voice as God-appointed prophets, speaking and advocating for God's purposes of reconciliation.

Another weakness of the fighting aggravator is that they are overly aggressive; rather than seeking to understand another perspective, they are only concerned with getting their viewpoint across. They don't heed the words of James: "Be quick to listen, slow to speak, and slow to anger" (James 1:19). They speak boldly what they believe is true, regardless of any other opinions or facts that would say otherwise. And even when they do hear the argument of another person, their only goal is to use it to better frame their own argument. They are not trying to actually understand or learn from anyone else.

While they may sometimes struggle with fatigue, fighting aggravators are not afraid to initiate. But the less and less they see change, the more aggressive they become. They aren't willing to stay the course for real and lasting change, which always takes a lot of patience, a lot of conversations, and a lot of time. Their aggression is a fear-filled response—they demand total change now and want to take matters into their own hands to ensure that change takes place. The issues they see so clearly are important, and their anger drives their passionate pursuit in these endeavors. But, without a heart toward reconciliation, their pursuits remain worldly.

Keep in mind, many Christians fall into this camp of aggravators (perhaps unknowingly). You'll see more in the following section, but don't write off this type of aggravator as for only those who don't know Christ. Many, in fact, see it as their faithful response to Christ—they are angry about the things that make him angry. They just don't always channel that anger toward reconciliation.

Many fighting aggravators have good reason to fight. Remember, one of their strengths can be their ability to see problems and call them out. And while the fighting aggravator may not be wrong in seeing the issues (or part of the issues) that divide, without the goal of reconciliation, rage, frustration, and further division will be the only results.

What Does the Bible Say?

If fighting aggravators don't want reconciliation, what do they want? Sometimes their goal is power or control. Sometimes it's validation. Sometimes it's revenge or punishment. Sometimes it's a short-sighted, incomplete version of justice. But without reconciliation, these goals fall short of grasping for what the gospel calls us toward. In so many ways, a fighting aggravator is like the prophetic voice of Jonah calling out truth to the Ninevites, all the while hoping for their destruction.

Another way I like to describe this type of aggravator is using the term "justified righteousness." You know in the movies when a man's daughter is kidnapped, and now suddenly we are all cheering for him to kill twenty other people to get his daughter back? When someone is wronged, we have the tendency to justify whatever behaviors are necessary to restore what was taken.

I'll admit, in the middle of a good movie, I'm inclined to cheer for this type of behavior. And when someone wrongs me, the temptation to respond out of justified righteousness is strong. But it's not the way of Christ. It's not the Christian way.

What did God have to say to Jonah's hard heart? When Jonah was furious because God spared the city, God asked him, "Is it right for you to be angry?" (Jonah 4:4). And then after God took away Jonah's shady plant, making Jonah angry again, look at their dialogue:

> "Then God asked Jonah, 'Is it right for you to
> be angry about the plant?'
>
> 'Yes, it's right!' he replied. 'I'm angry enough
> to die!'
>
> So the Lord said, 'You cared about the plant,
> which you did not labor over and did not grow.

> It appeared in a night and perished in a night.
> But may I not care about the great city of
> Nineveh, which has more than a hundred and
> twenty thousand people who cannot distinguish
> between their right and their left, as well as
> many animals?'" (Jonah 4:9–11)

And what does Jesus have to say to those who have been wronged?

> "You have heard that it was said, an eye for an
> eye and a tooth for a tooth. But I tell you, don't
> resist an evildoer. On the contrary, if anyone
> slaps you on your right cheek, turn the other to
> him also. As for the one who wants to sue you
> and take away your shirt, let him have your coat
> as well." (Matt. 5:38–40)

The tendency of the fighting aggravator is to take matters into their own hands, choosing their own way over God's way. Retribution and revenge are often key. Their language tends to be more revolutionary than reconciliatory. And this is not something the Lord takes lightly.

Doing things our own way and responding out of a sense of justified righteousness are symptoms of disbelief. A fighting aggravator struggles to believe that God will do what he promised, that God is good, that God's timing is perfect, and that God's way is best. A fighting aggravator ignores God's words in Deuteronomy 32:35, quoted by Paul in Romans 12:19: "Friends, do not avenge yourselves; instead, leave room for God's wrath, because it is written, 'Vengeance belongs to me; I will repay,' says the Lord."

I am *not*, as you'll soon see, saying passivity is the answer. And I am certainly not saying to let injustice run rampant. What I want to get at here is the posture of our hearts, the motivations for our actions, and the ways we trust (or don't trust) God. Fighting aggravators need to trust that God is just, that he will ultimately and finally act on the side of the oppressed, and that they are called, even in their work toward justice, to submit to the commands of Jesus.

A Fleeing Aggravator

PERCEIVED DANGER

The fleeing response is often triggered in the face of a danger that appears insurmountable. Whether it be from lack of resources or skills necessary to confront the danger, or whether it be simply from fear or lack of passion, running away looks like the best choice to remain safe. The fleeing response is also triggered in those who do not see an issue with the status quo—whether that is because they like things the way they are or they truly do not see any problems, they often hold the belief that divisions would disappear if we would just stop talking about them.

In response to issues of racial reconciliation, fleeing aggravators are passive. They certainly don't engage the problems with passion. Dr. Chip Dodd defines passion as "a willingness to endure the pain for something greater than the pain."[9] And for some fleeing aggravators, the pain of engaging in the divisions is not worth it. They do not have enough passion to endure the pain of pursuing reconciliation. For others, the changing of the status quo could be the very thing they perceive as most

---

[9] Chip Dodd, *Voice of the Heart*, 2nd ed. (Nashville, TN: Sage Hill, LLC, 2015).

dangerous (although this may not surface consciously or intentionally). Some may value public perception, and if they are in a place of comfort or power, anything that might change the status quo could be a threat to their way of life. They might also see the unrest that comes from conflict as dangerous because they value comfort over change. Their fear of loss is seen as a threat, whether it be loss of power, structures, authority, leverage, or friendships. Others do want to see a change, but they're so overwhelmed by the task at hand that they run away from the conflict.

One of the trickiest types of perceived dangers a fleeing aggravator might struggle with is actually not danger, but discomfort. In a compelling article, Robin DiAngelo explains how for those in the majority culture (and this concept would apply to anyone experiencing comfort and power from the status quo) who are so used to being comfortable, discomfort is often misinterpreted as something being "wrong."[10] For example, a White person who hasn't been in many minority-majority settings might feel unsafe sitting at a bus stop as the only White person. In reality, this person is merely uncomfortable. But whether because of messages in media, personal prejudices, a past experience, or other implicit biases, the person interprets the situation as dangerous.

This simple but profound principle also helps us understand why a fleeing aggravator might run from divisive race issues. Conflict can be uncomfortable. And if an "uncomfortable" trigger automatically triggers a sense of perceived danger, the flight response will quickly follow for the fleeing aggravator. And so, in this way, discomfort has become a type of perceived danger.

---

[10] Robin DiAngelo, p. 60 of *International Journal of Critical Pedagogy*, vol. 3 (3) (2011), 54–70, https://libjournal.uncg.edu/ijcp/article/viewFile/249/116.

STRENGTHS AND WEAKNESSES

Sometimes fleeing aggravators utilize the approach of color-blindness. In his book *Beyond Racial Gridlock*, Dr. George Yancey describes the approach:

> The core argument of the colorblindness model
> is simple: to end racism, we have to ignore racial
> reality. . . . If we emphasize racial issues, then
> we will continue to have racial problems. . . . If
> we only stop taking race into account, racism
> will lose its power to alienate people from each
> other. . . . The colorblind vision is of a society
> in which racial features such as skin color and
> facial structure are no more important than
> height or hair color. . . . If we can diminish the
> importance of race, then racial stratification
> and alienation will no longer be possible. . . .
> Colorblindness helps us correct the tendency of
> some racial minorities to look for racism where
> it does not exist.[11]

Yancey goes on to explain how Christians who adopt this model often do so out of a genuine desire to live under the eternal realities of the new identities that Christ purchased for us on the cross.[12] So, one of the strengths of a fleeing aggravator can be their focus on the eternal. They value the souls of people and tend to spend a lot of time engaging in deep thought and working on powerful spiritual concepts and matters of the heart.

---

[11] George Yancey, *Beyond Racial Gridlock: Embracing Mutual Responsibility* (Downers Grove, IL: InterVarsity Press, 2006), 29–30, 32.

[12] Ibid., 40.

This is a real strength, but it can be short-lived, as it is often based on a faulty understanding of racial divisions, and in turn, can be used as an excuse to avoid dealing with other difficult parts of society and life.[13] They hide behind Christianese language of living for eternity while ignoring the present realities around them.

The argument also falls apart when we recognize that we will not be colorblind throughout eternity. We will still be people from "every nation, tribe, people, and language" (Rev. 7:9). And Revelation portrays that as something to celebrate, something to see, something noticeable that will glorify God. Fighting for colorblindness in our lives today is not only contrary to the picture we see in Revelation, but it also puts you in danger of supporting the status quo—and supporting the status quo will always help those in power. Left unchecked, colorblindness only propagates oppression in our societies.

Many fleeing aggravators struggle with fragility when it comes to conversations and engagement with race and divisive issues. They prefer to not even start the conversation. They'd rather avoid anything that would challenge them to engage in this space and pretend like everything is fine. They're sick and tired of these conversations about racial divisions. But they're not tired because of how much they've engaged the issues—they're tired out of lack of practice.

Think about this in terms of athletics. Let's say you've got an Olympian athlete who trains eight hours a day, six days a week. This athlete experiences fatigue at the end of a work week. But it's a fatigue that came from long hours of muscle engagement and work. On the other hand, you may have a sedentary individual

---

[13] Ibid., 35, 39.

who works at a desk from 9–5 every day of the week. And for this person, just walking up two flights of stairs can be exhausting. This fatigue comes because this person's muscles have not been practiced. They are out of shape; their muscles are fragile. And in so many ways, a fleeing aggravator can be out of shape in regard to engaging division. As a result, the slightest mention of these issues causes immediate defense mechanisms to flare up.

Passivity is perhaps the greatest weakness of the fleeing aggravator. My good friend, brother, and fellow pastor, John Onwuchekwa says passivity occurs when "a love for self crowds out the ability to love others." Because of this love for self that blinds them to others, they tend to only view the problems of others through their own personal lens. But the thing about passivity is that it is driven by public perception. Passive people are not opinionless people; they simply value the opinions of others about them as the highest priority. If they think their opinions will hurt the way they are perceived or if they think there's no purpose, they will run. So while they may not voice many of these thoughts (except in environments with others who think just like them), they are often the driving force behind what is causing a fleeing aggravator to run away.

WHAT DOES THE BIBLE SAY?

The Bible is not without its own examples of fleeing aggravators. Look at Jacob in Genesis 34. His own daughter, Dinah, was raped, and Jacob did absolutely nothing about it. But after his sons deceived and killed the man guilty of rape, Jacob's heart became clear. He was angry with his sons and said to them, "'You have brought trouble on me, making me odious to the inhabitants of the land, the Canaanites and the Perizzites. We are few in number; if they unite against me and attack me, I and my household will be destroyed.' But they answered, 'Should he treat our sister like a prostitute?'" (vv. 30–31).

Jacob's concern was primarily for himself and how others might perceive him. And that love for self completely crowded out his ability to love his daughter well after she was raped. He was passive, choosing to run away from the issues rather than to engage. But his passivity only served to further aggravate the situation, as his sons responded by murdering the man.

Fleeing aggravators tend to believe one of three lies. On the one hand, some believe that if they run away from the problems, the problems will just stop being there. They believe the best way to deal with the problem is by not dealing with it, because there's really not that big of a problem anyway.

On the other hand, some believe the lie that the situation is hopeless. They run away from the problem because it's so bad that they don't think it could ever be fixed. Or finally, some believe the lie that it's not worth the pain, it's not worth the cost of pursuing reconciliation. But what none of these groups realize is that in running away, they are pouring more gasoline on the fire, and encouraging greater division, not healing and unity. Running away is not a neutral action.

In response to one fleeing aggravator's view of "save the soul, the rest will follow," the gospel also has much to say. And while we are commanded to live in light of eternity (2 Cor. 4:17–18; Col. 3:2; Matt. 6:19–20), the Bible never tells us to ignore the physical bodies and real-time needs of our neighbors and communities. In fact, it is quite the opposite. The book of James is filled from beginning to end with a defense for the importance of meeting real needs. In James 1:27, he writes, "Pure and undefiled religion before God the Father is this: to look after orphans and widows in their distress and to keep oneself unstained from the world." He goes on in James 2:15–16 to write, "If a brother or sister is without clothes and lacks daily food and one of you says to them, 'Go in peace, stay warm, and be well fed,' but you don't give them what the body needs, what good is it?"

The parable of the Good Samaritan is also a powerful indictment against passivity in the face of wounded humanity (Luke 10:25–37). Look at Jesus' final words to the experts in the law: "Which of these three do you think proved to be a neighbor to the man who fell into the hands of the robbers?' 'The one who showed mercy to him,' he said. Then Jesus told him, 'Go and do the same'" (Luke 10:36–37).

The very incarnation of Christ serves as evidence of God's concern for the needs of humanity. Jesus came and dwelt among a broken people. Yes, he spoke a message of hope. Yes, he chased after the souls of people. But he did not ignore broken bodies or hunger pains along the way. His willingness to heal on the Sabbath is perhaps one of the strongest proofs that Jesus did not see a disconnect between engaging human needs and fulfilling the spiritual law. Look at Mark 3:1–6.

> Jesus entered the synagogue again, and a man was there who had a shriveled hand. In order to accuse him, they were watching him closely to see whether he would heal him on the Sabbath. He told the man with the shriveled hand, "Stand before us." Then he said to them, "Is it lawful to do good on the Sabbath or to do evil, to save life or to kill?" But they were silent. After looking around at them with anger, he was grieved at the hardness of their hearts and told the man, "Stretch out your hand." So he stretched it out, and his hand was restored.

> Immediately the Pharisees went out and started
> plotting with the Herodians against him, how
> they might kill him.

While it may sound like good Christian lingo when a fleeing aggravator talks about prioritizing the eternal over the temporal, it may in reality be passivity in disguise. Look at what theologian and author John Stott once wrote,

> Our neighbor is neither a bodiless soul that we
> should love only his soul, nor a soulless body
> that we should care for its welfare alone; nor
> even a body-soul isolated from society. God
> created man, who is my neighbor, a body-
> soul-in-community. Therefore, if we love our
> neighbor as God made him, we must inevitably
> be concerned for his total welfare—the good of
> his soul, his body, and his community.[14]

A Frozen Aggravator

PERCEIVED DANGER

Frozen aggravators tend to be paralyzed by fear of change and/or fear of failure. If you think of the freezing response—like a possum playing dead—you can understand why freezing can be a completely natural response in the face of danger. But, in regard to issues of racial division, the freezing of this type of aggravator only serves to greater exacerbate the problem.

---

[14] John Stott and Christopher J. H. Rice, *Christian Mission in the Modern World*, updated and expanded ed. (Downers Grove, IL: InterVarsity Press, 2015), 29.

Frozen aggravators suffer from paralysis by analysis. They're so afraid they might do the wrong thing that they choose to do nothing at all. Sometimes frozen aggravators may be most aware of all the nuances of a situation, but the analysis of all the possible ways to offend and fail leads them to freeze in their tracks. For others, they may be so scared of change they freeze; too paralyzed to prevent it or move toward it, they just remain silent and disengaged.

At our old house, we used to keep our dog food outside. So one day I went outside to feed the dogs, and all of a sudden I saw something start to move. I realized it was a possum, and, showing me its teeth, it jumped out of the dog food container! The dogs went crazy and started barking at and attacking it. After it stopped moving, I assumed they had killed it. So I got the dogs to go inside and realized, *I've got to move this thing.* I started praying. *Lord, is he playing possum or is he really dead?* And you have to remember, I'm a city guy. I didn't know much about possums. But I'm looking at him laying there and there's stuff coming out of his mouth, so I'm freaking out, trying to figure out what I'm going to do with this dead thing. But I walked away for a minute, and when I came back, he was gone. (I later learned that they can emit things out of their mouths to make it seem more like they're dead.) More than any other animal, the "playing dead" response of the possum is probably most like the freezing response of a frozen aggravator.

Based on my experiences with my own church family and with other Christians I know, this is the category I believe most Christians fall into. Because I'm an optimist at heart, my assumption is that most people are here because they lack the tools to feel equipped to engage in a meaningful way. We know something is wrong, but we don't feel that we have the means to bring about the necessary changes. I agree with Emerson and

Smith that, too often, people with the deepest desires to see these divisions overcome end up contributing to the division because they lack the tools to engage well.[15]

STRENGTHS AND WEAKNESSES

Some frozen aggravators have a great strength in that they are very informed and aware of what is going on. They may read a lot or watch a variety of news sources or find other ways to engage the information. And this strength could be very helpful in crafting holistic plans for change. But due to their paralysis by analysis and feeling overwhelmed by the issues they see, their weakness steps in and they freeze in the face of division.

Another strength is that frozen aggravators have a healthy awareness of the possibility of offending others. They genuinely don't want to make the situation any worse, and don't want to offend other people involved. Unfortunately, of course, this strength is often exactly what leads them to inaction.

On the flip side, other frozen aggravators may be totally unaware of the nuances of the issues of division. They may see a problem, feel overwhelmed by the amount of work there is to be done, and freeze in response. And again, others may freeze due to fatigue. Some may be exhausted from working hard to see change and failing to see it, and then give up. Others may be tired because the divisions themselves seem too daunting to overcome.

Regardless of the reasons for freezing, the paralysis of a frozen aggravator produces a double think where their lifestyle doesn't match up with their stated values and beliefs. They likely have a genuine desire to see reconciliation, but their paralysis

---

[15] Michael Emerson and Christian Smith, *Divided by Faith* (Oxford University Press, 2001), 1.

produces passivity and their life in turn does not reflect a lifestyle of reconciliation.

In many ways, frozen aggravators are their own biggest threat. They think they are disqualified to engage because they lack the tools or qualifications. Or maybe they are distracted by other things that seem more important, or at least easier to address.

WHAT DOES THE BIBLE SAY?

When I think of frozen aggravators, I think of the way the early apostles related to Paul. They saw what was going on, they knew something needed to be done, but no one except Barnabas would engage with him. Another example is Peter in Galatians 2. Instead of addressing the issues with the Judaizers, he just stayed in the status quo, frozen, unwilling to engage. And we see how this paralysis led Peter to live in a way that didn't match with the values he claimed. Look at what Paul writes in Galatians 2:11–12:

> But when Cephas came to Antioch, I opposed
> him to his face because he stood condemned. For
> he regularly ate with the Gentiles before certain
> men came from James. However, when they
> came, he withdrew and separated himself, because
> he feared those from the circumcision party.

We can see it again in James 2:15–16 when James makes an indictment against those who stand idly by in the face of need. James concludes that this is ultimately a lack of faith. Regardless of the motives for freezing, the result of aggravating remains the same: division is deepened. Even those Christians who are frozen for the best of reasons are only further contributing to the issues that divide us. The driving force behind their response is not reconciliation, but fear. And any response that is not done with a heart for reconciliation is a response of an aggravator.

Maybe you find yourself relating to one type of aggravator. Or maybe you can see yourself in all three. I know for me, different situations can trigger different responses. No matter how you connect to these types of aggravators, just know you're not alone in these struggles because the fight, flight, or freeze responses are survival tactics wired in our brains.

The good news is, because we are in Christ, we are new creations (2 Cor. 5:17)! And we have the freedom to walk in our new identity and respond in godly ways because of Christ living within us. So let's turn from awareness (where are we?) to vision and look at where God wants us to be.

PART 2

WHERE DOES GOD WANT US TO BE?

CHAPTER 2

Vision

Over the past couple of years, the term *woke* has become a buzzword in many Christian and non-Christian settings. It carries with it the implication of someone who is awake, alert, and informed of the current events and injustices happening in our country, especially in regards to systemic racism and issues of racial division.[1]

In his poem "New Woke Christian," Preston Perry says, "To the Christian, there is nothing wrong with being woke. In fact, I believe when we care about injustice, heaven smiles with a grin of a thousand horizons." But he goes on to challenge our understanding of what it means to be woke. In this powerful spoken word, he asks and answers seven questions—questions that I believe challenge all three types of aggravators—casting

---

[1] Eric Mason, *Woke Church* (Chicago, IL: Moody Publishers, 2018), 25.

an incredible vision for what it means to be a *biblically* woke Christian.

Seven Questions to the Woke Christian (my paraphrase):

1. Are you really woke? Or just cold?
2. Is being woke only a trend for you?
3. Have you mistaken being woke with hatred?
4. Has your heritage and culture become your functional savior?
5. Do you think Christians should not be woke?
6. Are you hurting? Is it hard to do church when injustices are being swept under the pulpit?
7. Did you know Christ is a woke Jew from Galilee?[2]

We aren't going to go through the answers to his seven questions here, but I would encourage you to go to his website, prestonnperry.com, and watch Preston perform the "New Woke Christian." What I love about these questions and his poem is that they force us to consider current issues through a biblical lens.

And that's exactly the goal of this chapter. We don't simply want to respond out of a gut reaction. Because we know our guts are sinful and self-centered, we want to look to the Scriptures to find out what God's vision is for us. Who is he calling us to become?

I remember wrestling with the idea of vision throughout seminary. On one hand, I felt like the gospel provided compelling

---

[2] https://www.youtube.com/watch?v=imo0e0G8aF4

vision, and I began to feel consumed with a desire to see that vision come to reality. But on the flip side, I felt like I was walking back into a world and into a church culture that seemed impotent when it came to living out these gospel realities. And I remember really wrestling with these tensions and wanting to find a way to bridge the gap between what I saw in reality and what the Bible said should be. I came to a place where I told the Lord, "I just want to make church about you and your people, because it seems like it has become about everything else except that."

God has given us a clear and compelling vision for the church and how we are to live as Christians in a divided world. But instead of living out or even living in light of this vision, what I find is that we often live with *anti-vision*. As believers, we've gotten really good at painting pictures of what should *not* be, instead of living in a reality of what *should* be. We are way better at talking about what God is against than what God is actually for. And that's the difference between vision and anti-vision.

We need a holistic vision of a reconciled church because what we are currently operating under is mostly anti-vision. We have an anti-vision where we are more defined by what divides us than what unites us. We are more characterized by the adjective we place before the word *Christian* than we are characterized by simply being Christian. We have so many things that divide us: Calvinist Christian, Arminian Christian, rich Christian, poor Christian, city Christian, rural Christian, mega-church Christian, house-church Christian—the list could go on and on.

Perry's poem talks about this idea of a new vision for the new woke Christian, and he paints a compelling picture for us of what it can look like to be woke in the midst of a divided country. But before we go further, I think it's important to look at the Scriptures and ask if there is biblical precedent to being woke.

We've already seen in this book's preface that the Bible is clear on issues of justice. "He has told each of you what is good and what it is the LORD requires of you," Micah 6:8 says, "to act justly, to love faithfulness, and to walk humbly with your God." Proverbs 31:8 says, "Speak up for those who have no voice, for the justice of all who are dispossessed." Working for justice, then, is essential to a life of obedience; we cannot be obedient to Christ and ignore injustice.

Being woke is about being aware of the injustice that exists. In the twenty-first century United States, then, it is about being aware of racial injustice, inequity, and inequality based on race and ethnicity. How can we be awake to God's call to pursue justice if we have our eyes closed toward the injustice that exists?

But we can add to a biblical definition of *wokeness* by looking further in the Bible. Consider what Paul writes in Romans 13:11–14 (emphasis mine):

> Besides this, since you know the time, it is already the hour for you *to wake up* from sleep, because now our salvation is nearer than when we first believed. The night is nearly over, and the day is near; so let us discard the deeds of darkness and put on the armor of light. Let us walk with decency, as in the daytime: not in carousing and drunkenness; not in sexual impurity and promiscuity; not in quarreling and jealousy. But put on the Lord Jesus Christ, and don't make plans to gratify the desires of the flesh.

Wake up from sleep! For the Christian, being woke means to put on the Lord Jesus Christ, to walk as he walked—as reconcilers, ambassadors, and advocates in a divided world. When we put on Christ, we put on his identity and choose to engage how he would, not the way our flesh is inclined.

But this passage also adds a powerful dimension to our definition of wokeness not often seen in mainstream culture: culturally, being woke doesn't always provide boundaries for whether you are operating in the flesh or the Spirit, whether you are living in sin or in holiness. Paul calls us to "walk with decency . . . not in carousing and drunkenness; not in sexual impurity and promiscuity; not in quarreling and jealousy." Just as we need a holistic understanding of justice, we need a holistic understanding of biblical wokeness, one that includes awareness of systemic injustices in the world *and* a desire for personal holiness, one that brings the gospel to bear on social issues *and* on personal issues. To imitate Christ is to walk in personal holiness (not in carousing and drunkenness; not in sexual impurity and promiscuity) *and* to work toward reconciliation (not in quarreling and jealousy).

Some want to work toward justice without any regard for personal holiness. Others aren't truly seeking reconciliation but simply punishment. The disclaimers here for both of those groups are, first, to not make any plans to gratify the desires of the flesh, and second, that we are to walk in the light and discard the deeds of darkness. Paul makes it clear in this text that we are not to operate as if we don't have bumper rails or boundaries. We are to "put on the Lord Jesus Christ"! And I think one of the best concepts to describe what it means to "put on the Lord Jesus Christ" is to become advocates.

Look how John describes Jesus in 1 John 2:1. "My little children, I am writing you these things so that you may not sin. But if anyone does sin, we have an advocate with the Father—Jesus Christ the righteous one."

The writer of Hebrews uses the word *mediator* as a way to describe Jesus the Advocate in Hebrews 8:1–6:

> Now the main point of what is being said is this: We have this kind of high priest, who sat down at the right hand of the throne of the Majesty in the heavens, a minister of the sanctuary and the true tabernacle that was set up by the Lord and not man. For every high priest is appointed to offer gifts and sacrifices; therefore, it was necessary for this priest also to have something to offer. Now if he were on earth, he wouldn't be a priest, since there are those offering the gifts prescribed by the law. These serve as a copy and shadow of the heavenly things, as Moses was warned when he was about to complete the tabernacle. For God said, "Be careful that you make everything according to the pattern that was shown to you on the mountain." But Jesus has now obtained a superior ministry, and to that degree he is the mediator of a better covenant, which has been established on better promises.

And again in Hebrews 9:15: "Therefore, he is the mediator of a new covenant, so that those who are called might receive the promise of the eternal inheritance, because a death has taken place for redemption from the transgressions committed under the first covenant."

As our advocate, Christ reconciled us to the Father and made a way for us to be reconciled to one another. The command to put on Christ and live as he lived is given and echoed in many places throughout the New Testament. There is one small and particularly powerful example of putting on Christ in this way: the book of Philemon.

This short New Testament letter is where we will turn our primary focus for the rest of this book. Here, we see Paul clearly modeling the advocacy of Christ. We can learn from the principles we see clearly displayed in this book, while using Paul's other writings (primarily in 2 Corinthians) to validate and give further support to what we see in Philemon.

Division

My personal study of the book of Philemon started after the 2016 presidential election. On the night of election, I turned on the TV and saw all the political commotion. I was flipping through the channels and started to see the results come in. At first, it was kind of in the background as I casually flipped through different news channels. I quickly found myself being pulled into a vortex. Before I knew it, it was three o'clock in the morning and I had watched the news all night long. By this point, I couldn't stop. I was stunned. I had to see it, had to hear it. And finally, in the early hours of Wednesday morning, they made the official announcement.

As the news came in, I was wrecked with grief. However, as surprised as I was by President Trump's victory, I was most grieved not by who won the election, but by the phrase I kept hearing over and over again.

Our country is divided.
  Our country is divided.
    Our country is divided.

Christians were saying it. Nonbelievers were saying it. News anchors from every station were saying it. I heard those words ripple through every single news channel, and I was grieved to my core.

This election not only exposed the division that exists in our country, it exposed the division we have in the church. I talked to church members and watched social media channels to see how Christians were responding to the results. The more I talked with people and the more I read online, the more painfully clear the chasm within the American church became.

The reality hit close to home. I was faced with the fact that the church I pastor was divided. No longer was I wrestling with the far-off realities of a divided country—I had to turn and face the very present realities of my divided family.

One of the things the elders of Blueprint have said from the beginning is that we want to be a church in the city, like the city, for the city. And the reality is, the city is dense and the city is diverse. And when you have diversity of any kind, you're going to have diversity of opinions.

People on all sides of the spectrum had been vigilantly arguing to explain why their political opinion was the most Christian, the most just, the most "right." But unlike many people, I do not believe there was a strictly *evangelical* way to vote in this election. Faithful brothers and sisters interpreted the realities and the options different, and the result was a diversity of biblically justifiable options, with no clear biblically mandated option.

The problem is Christians generally do not know how to biblically deal with diverse opinions. In many ways, believers have responded to diverse opinions *worse* than the rest of the world. And in these responses, we see how a divided country exposes the tremendous division we have as a church. And as much as we want Blueprint to be a church for the city, in the city, that looks like the city, we also long to be a church who seeks and celebrates unity *within* our diversity. The 2016 election exposed just how difficult that would be.

From the time I was a kid and on into my early Christian years, whenever I was around African American Christians, I always heard the question, "How in the world can you be Christian and be Republican?" Then as I started studying at White evangelical institutions, I began to hear the *exact* opposite. People were asking, "How in the world can you be Christian and be a Democrat?" It was really interesting and disorienting to hear these polar opposite absolutes.

The connection here between race and opinion should not be underestimated. We often align more with our racial groups than with Christ. If Blueprint is really going to be a church in the city, for the city, that looks like the city, we had to begin to understand what *God* was calling us to be—not what our culture was demanding from us. And this is true for all Christians: *We must submit our cultural values to the values of Christ.*

Philemon

To address the divisions in our church, we stopped our sermon series and took a close look at the book of Philemon. Philemon is only one chapter long, but it is jam-packed with a clear example of a biblical advocate in action. Consider verses 1–3:

> Paul, a prisoner of Christ Jesus, and Timothy
> our brother: To Philemon our dear friend and
> coworker, to Apphia our sister, and Archippus
> our fellow soldier, and to the church that meets
> in your home. Grace to you and peace from
> God our Father and the Lord Jesus Christ.

Right here in the opening of the book, we see Paul addressing Philemon, a wealthy and godly man. Philemon was a man
who opened up his home for the sake of the church. You need to
understand, during that time, especially in times of persecution,
a lot of Christianity was dependent on the wealthy. The church
relied on wealthy families with larger homes to have space for the
church to gather together, and this was the case with Philemon.
The local church was gathering in his home.

In the beginning of the letter, Paul reaches out to him and
greets him warmly as someone he knows and loves—his fellow coworker. Paul and Philemon shared a partnership in the
gospel. And right from the beginning of the letter, Paul begins
to address the issue at hand. Ultimately, Paul is going to ask
Philemon to accept Onesimus.

Onesimus was a former slave of Philemon's who ran away,
ended up in prison, and was converted to Christianity through
the influence of Paul. And now, Paul is sending Onesimus back
to Philemon. But he is going to ask Philemon not to receive
Onesimus as a bondservant. Paul is asking Philemon to receive
him as a *brother*. Paul jumps right into the heart of the letter
and, in doing so, gives us a look at three key principles of being
advocates.

Before we dive into the three principles, I pray that you hear
my heart in the same way Philemon would have heard Paul's. If
you are reading this book, there is a good chance we don't know

each other personally. But if you are a follower of Jesus Christ, I am writing this to you as your brother and fellow coworker in the gospel. I long for you to hear from God's Word and learn practical tools to help bring unity in the midst of division, to help us learn how to become advocates within the body of Christ.

I know the divides in our churches can seem overwhelming. Racial tensions are high, wounds run deep, and there are unhealed offenses that are centuries old. In spite of this, I want to encourage you to jump in with your whole heart. This fight is not hopeless. We serve a God who conquered sin. He is the Healer. Through Christ, we can jump into the pit of racial division, into the divides that plague our local churches, and know with full confidence that we will not be overcome by the darkness of the divide.

No divide is deeper than the reaches of God's love. And that means no divide is so deep, no chasm so wide, that it cannot be unified through the love of Christ.

So as we explore Philemon in the coming chapters, I pray that you will study the Scriptures for yourself, that you will approach God's Word with humility, and that you will allow the Holy Spirit to change you through the truths of His Word.

As a brief note, Philemon is a very short book with only one chapter. So when we refer to different verses in Philemon without the chapter number, it's because there's only one! For the most part, these points will flow in order of the text, with the exception of a couple of verses being grouped under the first point. The three major points that we are going to see in this text are that an advocate:

1. Relies on Christ
2. Runs to the tension
3. Responds with dignity

CHAPTER 3

Advocates Rely on Christ

We Must Rely on Christ through Prayer

The very first thing Paul did as an advocate was pray. And this is exactly what we are called to do as advocates. *We must rely on Christ through prayer.*

In Philemon 4–7, Paul writes this:

> I always thank my God when I mention you
> in my prayers, because I hear of your love for
> all the saints that you have in the Lord Jesus.
> I pray that your participation in the faith may
> become effective through knowing every good
> thing that is in us for the glory of Christ. For I
> have great joy and encouragement from your

love, because the hearts of the saints have been
refreshed through you, brother.

In times of turmoil, Christians have a couple of go-to
responses. One of those is the simple reminder, "God is on his
throne." That was the most common response I heard from
Christians during and after the 2016 presidential election. And
that is absolutely true. He is still on the throne.

But the reality is, while we may *know* that God is on the
throne, we don't often live like that's true. Think about it.
Whenever there are problems or tragedies, we tend to go to
someone and say, "Tell me what to do. Yeah, yeah, I know I need
to pray. But then what?"

When we make that statement, we are saying yes, we *know*
God is on the throne, but we don't live like he really is. If we
really believe we serve a God who is all-powerful, all-knowing,
kind, and has the whole world in His hands—what more *can* we
do than pray to the One who can turn the heart of the king?
(Prov. 21:1).

Prayer is not just the first thing to get out of the way so we
can get to the real work. First and foremost, it *is* the real work.

Paul bookends this entire letter with prayer. He starts in
verse 4 and tells Philemon he is praying for him, and he ends in
verse 25 by asking for prayer. Paul undoubtedly believed in the
power of prayer. And it's a belief we see running throughout all
of Scripture.

In Matthew 9, Jesus commands us to pray to the Lord of the
harvest. He tells us that the harvest is plentiful but the laborers
are few—and our first command is to respond with prayer, to
pray for more laborers. Jesus does not command us to first go
train more laborers. Jesus commands us to pray.

In Philippians 4, Paul says, (and I paraphrase) "If you're anxious, you need to pray! Let your requests be made known to God and he will give you a peace that surpasses all understanding." Second Chronicles 7:14 tells us to humble ourselves and pray! To humble ourselves, we have to understand that we're not the solution; God is. So the first thing we need to do is pray to the One who *is* the solution.

Prayer is important because it allows us to place our fears in the right place. Feeling the emotion of fear is unavoidable in the midst of turmoil and conflict because fear is simply an emotion that lets us know we aren't in control.[1] But when you fully understand fear, you learn how it can lead to greater faith. As we recognize we aren't in control, we can rest because we know someone who is. I am able to turn and give all of my fear to the One who can actually do something with it.

Children are scared all the time. On a regular basis I hear my kids say, "Dad, I'm afraid of the dark. Dad, I don't want to go to the basement. Dad, I don't want to go by myself, I'm too scared." How do we see kids deal with their fear? What's their solution? Over and over again my kids will say, "Dad, I'm afraid of the dark. But if you'll come with me, I'll go." The presence of a trusted parent or friend eases the fear for children because they trust the adult to control the situation. This is what prayer helps us do.

Prayer allows us to remember where real power lies, that we have a Father who is in control of all things. If God is for us, who can stand against us? Prayer allows us to remember who has the ultimate authority.

---

[1] Chip Dodd, *Voice of the Heart*, 2nd ed. (Nashville, TN: Sage Hill, LLC, 2015).

Prayer also slows us down, giving us the ability to respond rather than react. I really believe it's important for us to pray because often when we operate out of our emotions, we end up saying and doing things we later regret. But when we sit down, slow down, process, and pray, we can reflect and take time to remember *whose* we are and what he's up to in the world. It helps us understand that we don't have to just react out of our emotions; prayer allows us to slow down so we can respond out of obedience.

We must recognize and embrace prayer for all that it is—not as an afterthought, not as a prelude in our actions, not as a ritual, but as the very means by which we are able to make our requests known to a powerful God. If we are going to be reconcilers, if we are going to be advocates, we must be on our knees, praying like our family is on the line—because it is!

Think of the types of things you would pray for in your marriage or your relationship with parents or siblings. Even though you know you won't always see eye to eye on an issue, you pray that God would give you the grace, courage, and stamina to stay in the fight. We should do the same here. We should pray that even when your opinions couldn't be more different, 1 Corinthians 13 would remain true—that we would embody a love that endures all things, hopes all things, and is able to stick it out in the midst of differences.

That is Paul's prayer in context—that Onesimus and Philemon would stay and fight for unity and not run away from the tension or from one another. We can't do this alone. We need Christ. And that is why we must rely on him through prayer.

We Must Rely on Christ through the
Full Knowledge of God's Grace

Another way we rely on Christ is *through the full knowledge of God's grace*. In verse 6 Paul says this: "And I pray that the sharing of your faith may become effective for the full knowledge of every good thing that is in us for the sake of Christ" (ESV). We see within this verse that Paul is praying more than a generic prayer. He is praying specifically for an understanding of the *full* knowledge of everything that is in us for the glory of Christ. The term *full knowledge* comes from the Greek word *epignosis*, that implies full or thorough discernment.[2] Paul is saying that as believers, we can know Christ in different ways. One way that we can know him is through our intellect. We can know his grace intellectually. We can understand his love, his mercy, and his power. But he is also reminding us that there is another type of knowledge. And especially in times of trials, conflict, and reconciliation, it is critical for us to know God and his grace intellectually, yes, but also experientially. Paul is talking about an *intimate* knowledge. We must strive for this full knowledge of the grace of God both intellectually and experientially.

When we begin to become advocates and put ourselves in harm's way in pursuit of reconciliation, it allows us to know the grace of God in our life experience. As Paul is praying, he prays for them to understand God in his fullness. Why? Because he is about to ask Philemon to do something that will require a lot from him. Paul is setting him up! He wants Philemon to remember that it's not just about knowing the right things, thinking the right things, or saying the right things. It's about *being* the right

---

    2   http://www.bibletools.org/index.cfm/fuseaction/Lexicon.show/ID /G1922/epignosis.htm

thing. Paul wants both Onesimus and Philemon to know the full knowledge of God's grace in thought *and* in real-time action.

Intellectual cognition alone does not equate with true or full knowledge. Jesus did not consider that his disciples knew something until they were able and willing to live it out, to obey what they knew. Robert E. Coleman writes in his book *The Master Plan of Evangelism*, "Jesus expected the men he was with to obey him. They were not required to be smart, but they had to be loyal. This became the distinguishing mark by which they were known."[3] We must not get trapped in a mere intellectual understanding of God and his extravagant grace. We must dive deep into the full knowledge of his grace, which requires that we practice it and experience his power outside of our individual quiet times. If we can discuss God's grace, write a paper on God's grace, and defend every theological nuance of it, but we cannot extend grace to our neighbor, then we know *nothing* of God's grace. We must engage with God and his grace in our relationships with other believers, with our neighbors, and with our cities.

Grace is not just unmerited favor; it's also divine enablement. Paul prays for Philemon to know the fullness of God's grace because he knows Philemon will need supernatural, enabling power to pursue reconciliation with Onesimus. Look at the following Scriptures and pay close attention to the ways grace is seen as enabling power, as something active that grows and moves.

---

[3] Robert E. Coleman, *The Master Plan of Evangelism*, 2nd ed. (Grand Rapids, MI: Revell, 1993), 49.

> With great power the apostles were giving testi-
> mony to the resurrection of the Lord Jesus, and
> great grace was on all of them. (Acts 4:33)

> . . . but grow in the grace and knowledge of our
> Lord and Savior Jesus Christ. (2 Pet. 3:18)

> And God is able to make every grace overflow
> to you, so that in every way, always having
> everything you need, you may excel in every
> good work. (2 Cor. 9:8)

To be an advocate means that we are walking in the enabling power of God's grace and applying it to the brokenness of our human relationships. In this endeavor toward reconciliation, theological understanding will not take us very far. The *application* of grace, the application of love, the application of truth is what will bridge the divides—not just the knowledge of it.

But we cannot give something we do not have. Therefore, if we have not experienced the fullness of God's grace, how can we give it to others? Only when we start to experience God in real-time will we begin to engage with the full knowledge of God's grace that is required for an advocate. As we walk in obedience we will be met with the magnificent grace of our Father, and those experiences will empower us to offer that same grace to others.

There are times when I am afraid we have turned Christianity into an intellectual religion. Don't get me wrong—God created our intellect, and he wants us to study, to be astute, and to be able to speak intelligently about who he is and what his Word says. In fact, we can't know God experientially if we don't know him intellectually. This is what Paul says in Romans 10 of his fellow Jews: "I can testify about them that they have zeal for

God, but not according to knowledge. Since they are ignorant of the righteousness of God and attempted to establish their own righteousness, they have not submitted to God's righteousness" (Rom. 10:2–3). To have zeal for God but to be ignorant of God's righteousness is to fail to submit to God.

But there's a flip side of the coin. Like James, I often want to ask other Christians, "What good is it, my brothers and sisters, if someone claims to have faith but does not have works?" (James 2:14). What good is it to know of God's grace and then fail to apply it? Indeed, faith that is only intellectual and does not play out in good works, James says, is dead. If we don't obey Jesus, it's proof that we are not really Christians.

Paul knows he is about to ask Philemon to walk a path toward reconciliation that is not possible for humans to do alone. To bridge these divides, to truly reconcile with one another, we must rely on Christ through the *full* knowledge of God's grace, both in intellect and in experience.

We see a similar principle in 2 Corinthians where Paul shares how advocates are motivated by experiencing the love of Christ as Savior. He writes in 2 Corinthians 5:14–15, "For the love of Christ compels us, since we have reached this conclusion: If one died for all, then all died. And he died for all so that those who live should no longer live for themselves, but for the one who died for them and was raised." Other translations of these verses interpret the word for *compels* as *controls*.[4] That word carries a lot of weight in this verse. The love of Christ controls, compels, constrains, guides, motivates, and leads the words and actions of an advocate. Why? Because when we are in Christ, we

---

[4] See the NASB translation.

have exchanged our life for his. This is evident throughout all of Paul's life and ministry.

Let's look at 1 Corinthians 9. Paul states clearly in the opening verses of the chapter that as an apostle of Christ Jesus, he has certain rights. He concludes his argument in verse 11 by saying, "If we have sown spiritual things for you, is it too much if we reap material benefits from you?" But he quickly adds, "Nevertheless, we have not made any use of this right; instead, we endure everything so that we will not hinder the gospel of Christ" (1 Cor. 9:12). And not only did he not demand his rights as an apostle, he gave up more of his rights, making himself a slave to all people in order to win more people (1 Cor. 9:19).

The language Paul uses here is strong. *Becoming a slave. Giving up rights. Enduring everything.* And yet, doesn't this sound just like our Savior? When we are in Christ, we exchange our life for his. And that is abundantly evident in Paul's life. Paul was motivated by Christ as Savior because he knew (both intellectually and experientially) the love of God and the grace of God, and that motivation led him to let go of his rights and be entirely compelled and controlled by the love of Christ. This is the motivation that burned in him, that created a deep desire to see others know Christ in the same way.

Paul concludes in 1 Corinthians 9:23 by saying, "Now I do all this because of the gospel, so that I may share in the blessings." And my question to us today is, do we still consider the gospel a blessing? Can we honestly say that our actions and words are controlled by the love of Christ? Because if they were, there would be no heights or depths that would keep us from fighting to be reconciled with one another.

We Must Rely on Christ by Recognizing God's Providence

Another way advocates rely on Christ is by recognizing the providence of God. Jump down with me to Philemon 15 where Paul writes, "For perhaps this is why he was separated from you for a brief time, so that you might get him back permanently." Paul recognizes the providence of God—God's intentional, loving action in orchestrating events for a purpose—in the midst of this situation.

I don't think it is by chance that we live in the most urban generation in the history of man.[5] But I also don't think it's by chance that we have seen some of the most wicked crimes and are experiencing some of the greatest tension in the history of man. Do you know that we are living during the largest recorded refugee crisis in the history of the world?[6] Do you realize that we are in a time where warfare doesn't even catch us off guard anymore? We live in a time where we are becoming increasingly jaded to gun violence. "Oh, another Black person got shot by a cop. Oh, there was another school shooting this week. Oh, there was another shootout at the park." And that only scratches the surface of some of the tensions our neighborhoods are dealing with.

Do you realize the amount of tension that exists in our world? In our cities? Don't be blind to it. It's easy to be intentionally ignorant. It's tempting to turn off the news, or to become totally numb to the tensions around us. Don't give in to that temptation.

But once we realize the depth of these tensions and the gravity of the issues, then what? Should we just resort to fear? No, we

---

[5] Mark Gottdiener and Ray Hutchison, *New Urban Sociology*, 4th ed. (Boulder, CO: Westview Press, 2010), 21.

[6] https://www.unhcr.org/figures-at-a-glance.html

should continue to rely on Christ and view these tensions in light of our God who has all things in control.

Maybe he is aligning all these things because he has something to say to the church. Or maybe he is aligning all these things because he has something to say *through* the church. Perhaps God is allowing our brokenness to become painfully clear so that we would be forced to unite in Christ—the only possible way we can have unity within diversity.

Remember how Mordecai encouraged Esther in the midst of the racial tensions arising during her time? Esther was hesitant to go before the king, knowing that to do so would be to risk her life. Mordecai challenged her and said, "If you keep silent at this time, relief and deliverance will come to the Jewish people from another place, but you and your father's family will be destroyed. Who knows, perhaps you have come to your royal position for such a time as this" (Esther 4:14). Like Esther, we too must not underestimate God's providence. Perhaps you and I were placed here for such a time as this.

Too often, instead of responding with faith and trust in God, we respond with fear, passivity, and anger. We allow our emotions to dictate our response and in turn become aggravators instead of advocates. We see all throughout Scripture how God often allows darkness to come so that the light can shine brighter, clearer, and farther than before. If we are too busy fighting for our position or rights or opinions, we will get trapped in a fight for our own glory and miss our ultimate calling to fight for the glory of God. We will not be able to respond to the events of the world with faith and trust in God if we lose focus, if we lose sight of his providence in the midst of our brokenness. Taking time to pause and remember the truths of God's character and his control in our situations, taking time to recognize his providence, is a powerful practice that helps us continue to trust him and rely on him as we live as advocates.

We Must Rely on Christ by Revering Him and His Work

The last way we see Paul rely on Christ is through revering the person and work of Christ. It may seem subtle, but look at how this letter starts and ends. In verse 1, Paul begins by introducing himself as "Paul, a prisoner of Christ Jesus." And his last words in verse 25 are, "The grace of the Lord Jesus Christ be with your spirit." Not only in these words, but in his actions throughout the letter, Paul is demonstrating how he relies on Christ through his reverence.

One way we rely on Christ by revering what he has done is by recognizing that we aren't the solution to these problems. Christ is. And the more we can embody the person and work of Christ through the power of his Spirit, taking less of ourselves and more of him, advocating for his way, seeking after his will, the more we will be able to see the grace of the Lord displayed.

Paul is ultimately saying that all relationships within the church are regarded through the framework of the person and work of Christ. We are *in* Christ. And if we are not able to solve the issues *within* the church and the animosity and the tension we have *in* the church, then we really don't have anything to offer anyone else. We haven't quite gotten there in the narrative, but here's a little spoiler alert: Paul tells the offended Philemon, rather than solely seeking punitive-justice, to receive Onesimus as a reconciled sibling because of Christ's work in him. He says to the offender, Onesimus, even though he could have had an easier way out, he needs to go back.

We see in Scripture where God instructs us to stop offering things to him when we know we have a brother who has a sin against us. We need to return to that brother, reconcile, and then go back to the altar (Matt. 5:23–24). Paul tells Onesimus to go back to Philemon because his brother has a sin against him. But just because he's going back doesn't mean there won't be consequences. Paul is saying, "No, accept that there may be consequences for your actions. You may have to fulfill the obligations." Yet, it is still only because of Christ's work that we are able to accept the consequences and continue to walk toward reconciliation.

As a church, we *must* become better advocates. When we see disobedience happening, when we see division, we cannot watch passively. Grace isn't passive. This world is on a conveyer belt going the opposite way from where Christ wants us to go. For us to do nothing is to get pulled along with the world. Passive disobedience is active rebellion. And if we are passive, we are just as guilty as the propagators, the promoters, the aggravators of evil. And you see, this is why we need an advocate just as much as we need to be advocates. The beauty of it all is that we don't do this in our own power! We are relying on Christ. And in his grace, God has given us an Advocate. Remember the kind words in 1 John 2:1–2, where John writes, "My little children, I am writing these things to you so that you may not sin. But if anyone does sin, we have an advocate with the Father, Jesus Christ the righteous. He is the propitiation for our sins, and not for ours only but also for the sins of the whole world."

The Bible is very clear. It's not whether or not we are going to have conflict—we are going to have conflict. The question is, *Are we going to become advocates by first relying on the one who is advocating for us?* As believers, this is what it means when

Scripture says we don't wrestle with the darkness as those with-out hope (1 Thess. 4:13). Because we know that we have hope. And guess what? We aren't always going to do things the right way. But we have an Advocate with the Father, an Advocate who constantly says, "You aren't perfect, but I covered that. I died for you. And I am with you."

This is the very essence of our call to be reconcilers. We advocate for others to the point that we are willing to take on their burdens with and sometimes for them. We are willing to, like Jesus, endure pain and suffering for the good of our brothers and sisters—even those who are different from us. The church must, *must* become better advocates. If we align ourselves more with our political parties, our cultural background, our prefer-ences, or our race more than we do with the church, and we start fighting within the family, we begin to embrace what the Bible calls the spirit of anti-Christ (1 John 2:18–27; 4:2–3).

God has given us the ministry of reconciliation, and any-thing outside of trying to reconcile men back to God and back to one another is the spirit of anti-Christ. If we are divisive, we are working against God. Of course, the truth of the gospel is a dividing truth (see Matt. 10:34). But the gospel creates a divid-ing line between God's family and the world—not within God's family. The gospel unites, and within God's family, there should be no other divisions, because Jesus "tore down the dividing wall of hostility" (Eph. 2:14).

In 2 Corinthians, Paul displays this same reverence for Christ as he recognizes that he is accountable to Christ as Lord. In verse 11, Paul identifies two motives for Christian service: an awareness of our accountability to God and our attempt to take every opportunity to persuade people to trust Christ. We are both accountable to God as our Lord and we are to be active in persuading people to accept us as his ambassadors, which is hard because doing things God's way is not always the most appealing to the flesh, or to others. These two ideas—being accountable to the Lord and desiring to persuade others—are tied together by the fear of the Lord.

Look what the Bible says in Proverbs 9:10. "Fear of the LORD is the beginning of wisdom, and knowledge of the Holy One is understanding." In general, wisdom simply means applied knowledge. As believers, a lot of times we have knowledge, but we lack the wisdom for how to *apply* what we know. Another way to understand the fear of the Lord is to think of it as a healthy reverence for the Lord. To revere someone is to hold them in high regard, to esteem them, to think of them in a kind of awe-struck way. Fearing the Lord is not driven by fear of punishment, but by our reverence for him and an understanding of the protection he provides. When we revere the Lord, when we fear him and allow that fear to help guide our decisions, it helps us remember and keep in step with the types of decisions and actions God would have us make.

In Matthew 10, Jesus talked about fearing God. He told his disciples, "Don't fear those who kill the body but are not able to kill the soul; rather, fear him who is able to destroy both soul and body in hell" (Matt. 10:28). Why did Jesus say that? Was he trying to make his disciples run from God? No, *he was teaching them not to be scared of people.*

Right before Jesus said this, he commissioned the disciples to go and do ministry, and he warned them that they would meet enemies along the way. There would be people and situations that would make them afraid. And this is one of the reasons we live as aggravators—because we're scared of what would happen to us is if we became advocates! But Jesus is telling us, "Don't be afraid of the response you'll get for speaking truth. Don't be afraid of what people will do to you if you stand up with and for your brothers and sisters. Don't fear those who can socially alienate you or slander you or accuse you; fear God, who is Lord."

Jesus closes this section by saying to his disciples, "Aren't two sparrows sold for a penny? Yet not one of them falls to the ground without your Father's consent. But even the hairs of your head have all been counted. So don't be afraid; you are worth more than many sparrows" (vv. 29–31). Here we see that when we fear God instead of people, we're given a hedge of protection. God is to be feared, but because we know his character, our fear leads us toward greater faith as we trust him as our loving Father[7] to protect us as we become advocates, regardless of what the earthly consequences might be.

Our second motive is our desire to persuade people to believe. In his book, *Ordination Addresses and Counsels to Clergy*, J. B. Lightfoot writes, "The ambassador's duty is not merely to deliver a definite message, to carry out a definite policy; but he is obligated to watch opportunities, to study characters, to cast about for expedients, so that he may place it before his hearers in its most attractive form. He is a diplomatist."[8] And we recognize, even from our own experience, that when we are trying to persuade someone, context matters. In order for us to be effective, persuasive advocates, contextualization is key. You can't just have the same one-line speech you give to every person regardless of who they are, where they're from, or what their personal questions are. To persuade effectively, we must contextualize our message and presentation to meet the needs of our audience.

---

[7] Dodd, *Voice of the Heart*.

[8] J. B. Lightfoot, *Ordination Addresses and Counsels to Clergy* (London and New York: Macmillan, 1891), 47–48.

Simply stated, contextualization is communicating in a way that allows the receiver to receive the message in his or her heart's language while maintaining the integrity of the content.[9]

We can see Paul clearly explaining how he contextualized the gospel from his words in 1 Corinthians 9:19–22:

> Although I am free from all and not anyone's
> slave, I have made myself a slave to everyone,
> in order to win more people. To the Jews, I
> became like a Jew, to win the Jews; to those
> under the law, like one under the law—though
> I myself am not under the law—to win those
> under the law. To those who are without the
> law, like one without the law—thought I am not
> without God's law but under the law of Christ—
> to win those without the law. To the weak I
> became weak, in order to win the weak. I have
> become all things to all people, so that I may by
> every possible means save some.

And look again at 1 Timothy 1:5 where Paul writes, "Now the goal of our instruction is love that comes from a pure heart, a good conscience, and a sincere faith." Can you imagine if every time we engaged issues of racial division, our goal was to convince people to fall more in love with God and more in love with his people? Would that change the way we speak? The way we fight? Of course it would. And advocates recognize this because they live as those who will be held accountable to Christ. This transforms the way they engage systems and the way they engage people; it holistically impacts their interactions.

---

[9] Marvin J. Newell, *Crossing Cultures in Scripture: Biblical Principles for Mission Practice* (Downers Grove, IL: InterVarsity Press Books, 2016), 235.

CHAPTER 4

Advocates Run to the Tension

In Philemon verses 8–11 we see our second principle of being an advocate: *Advocates run into the tension of injustice.*

> For this reason, although I have great boldness in Christ to command you to do what is right, I appeal to you, instead, on the basis of love. I, Paul, as an elderly man and now also as a prisoner of Christ Jesus, appeal to you for my son, Onesimus. I became his father while I was in chains. Once he was useless to you, but now he is useful both to you and to me.

Instead of acting like there's only a *potential* for injustice to take place, Paul runs into the tension and he says, "Listen, Philemon. I understand the beef you have with Onesimus. And you know what? You're justified in that beef." And while Paul may acknowledge that Philemon is justified, he does not use it as an excuse to further the division.

Paul's saying to Philemon, "Listen, there's injustice here and there's the potential for more injustice, so I'm going to run to the tension where you are going to think you are justified. After all, Onesimus was a runaway slave! He did you wrong. And you know what, Roman law actually says that you can severely punish him.[1] But there's a new reality that we have in Christ, a new law." Paul runs straight to the tension and becomes an advocate for Onesimus.

We need to understand that whenever there is animosity or strife, whether in our families, neighborhoods, or nation, we cannot remain silent. I will say it again: *passive disobedience is active rebellion.* When our country is divided, we can't just sit around and act like nothing is happening. We must deal with the elephant in the room.

Regardless of how you voted, you've got to recognize that too often political leaders perpetuate their ideas by perpetuating fear. And even when they aren't explicitly using this strategy, one person's proposed political actions can trigger deep fear in someone who disagrees with their methods and policies. So no matter where you fall on the political spectrum, you've got to understand there is a lot of real fear plaguing people in our nation.

To try to act like we don't have anything to fear and then refuse to run to the tension is anti-Christian. Advocates must run to the tension. In conflict, a lot of times when the offender is ready to be done with the situation they just kind of bury their head in the sand and say, "Time heals all wounds. We don't have to address it any further. Let's just let time heal it." On the flip

---

[1] http://www.bbc.co.uk/history/ancient/romans/slavery_01.shtml

side, the offended has a tendency to fight for punitive-justice at all costs. And in this pursuit, the offended throws all other values out the window. But that's just rage. Not justice. The response of an advocate is to recognize the injustice and call it out. We have to call out the elephant in the room. We have to address it.

Let me make a quick qualifier here. You can't respond or give an answer for every issue or problem in the world. There's a reason I don't wake up and try to address the issues going on in countries halfway around the world. It's not because I don't care. It's because I can't! There's no way any person can even know about all the issues of the world, much less spend enough time to effectively engage in pursuing justice in all of them. So the question becomes, how do you determine the scope of the issues that you need to address? The way I tend to think about it is like this: it's not a real problem until it's your problem. And issues become real for you in two ways: *proximity* and *relationship*. Let me explain.

I live across the street from a park that has had multiple shootings. Before I moved into the neighborhood, I was concerned about that issue, but it wasn't my problem. Once I moved in and the stray bullets started flying into windows next door and my kids are hunkered down in the bathroom crying—now it's my problem. Why? Proximity. It's close to me. It directly impacts my life and the life of my family.

The other way problems become your own is through relationship. Let's say you have a problem with a coworker. That problem isn't mine to deal with. But now let's say my wife has a problem with a coworker. Because I love my wife and care deeply about what's going on in her life, this problem is now my own.

No matter where you live, your community has problems—both individual and systemic—because our cities are filled with broken people who created broken systems! Until we get to heaven, we will always live among brokenness. And if you don't feel like the problems are your own, then it probably means that you aren't close enough to the problem (proximity) or you aren't in deep enough relationship with those who are most impacted by the problems (relationship). Being a good neighbor doesn't just mean engaging with the people you normally have conversations with, but like the Good Samaritan, being willing to engage the people and issues of those God puts in your path.

So to the person who feels overwhelmed by all the problems you see, I hope this encourages you to know that it's okay to focus on the problems God has put you closest to. And for the person who doesn't feel connected to the problems at all, I hope you are encouraged to find ways to get closer to the issues and to engage in deeper relationships with people who don't look like you, act like you, or talk like you.

We must be willing to uphold God's standard of justice, to discuss the messy things, and to engage in the tension with all the complexities it may bring. Running to the tension may look like having a courageous conversation or challenging a friend or mediating between two parties or fighting for systemic change in a particular area of injustice. There are many different ways God might lead you to run into the tension, but the key factor of an advocate is the posture of our hearts. We will never live out our true identity as advocates if we fail to run into the tension of injustice.

God's Idea of Justice

I recognize that it's easy to talk about the idea of an advocate going into hostile situations and seeking to bring peace. But if you've been hurt by injustice and seen the damage it can do, it can make it difficult to keep your eyes on reconciliation when what you really want is punishment. But Paul encourages us to look back to the cross. "He made the one who did not know sin to be sin for us, so that in him we might become the righteousness of God" (2 Cor. 5:21).

Jesus Christ became sin for us so that we might become the very righteousness of God. This is God's idea of justice. And if we are going to be advocates, we must fight for God's justice and not our own.

This is not a call to sweep injustice under the rug—because that is not at all what God has done. But we must be willing to surrender our personal understanding and ideas of what justice is in order to pursue the type of justice God desires.

So let's look a little more closely at this. What does it mean that Jesus became sin for us? Well, first it means that God treated Jesus as if he were a sinner. When God poured out his wrath on Jesus, he bore the guilt and penalty of all peoples' sin. Jesus is sinless. This is clear to us throughout all of the Scriptures. But Jesus became sin because of us.

This also means that Jesus became our substitution. We recognize that we were totally unjust before God. The Bible says that we were enemies toward God (Rom. 5:10), but "God proves his own love for us in that while we were still sinners, Christ died for us" (Rom. 5:8). He was our substitution. "He himself bore our sicknesses, and he carried our pains; . . . he was pierced because of our rebellion, crushed because of our iniquities" (Isa. 53:4–5). God poured out his wrath (that we deserve) on Christ.

And that's the important point here. God is just and he must punish sin. But in his great love, he didn't want to punish us and be separated from us forever. So because of that, because of the person and work of Jesus, God now treats imperfect humans as if we are perfect. He is just (in punishing sins) and the justifier (in giving us the righteousness of Christ) (Rom. 3:26).

Do you see the beauty of the gospel? God first treated Jesus, the one with no sin, as a sinner. But at the end, he now treats us, who are full of sin as if we are sinless! Jesus was the recipient of God's punishment for sinners. God transferred the sin account of all of humanity to Christ. And now, God makes us the recipients of his righteousness, transferring the righteous account of Jesus to all who have faith in him. This is good news. The amazing effect of God giving us Christ's righteousness is that God sees us as people who have been fully reconciled to him.

This good news reveals to us the weight of the responsibility of God's ambassadors. Whenever we come into these situations, environments, or conversations where there is injustice, we must arise out of our sleep, make no provisions for the flesh, and recognize that God's ministry is reconciliation. When we embrace our role as his ambassadors, we must recognize that we speak as those who speak on behalf of Christ, as those who live on behalf of Christ, as those who embody the very DNA of Christ who has reconciled the world to himself, and as those who are truly advocate ambassadors of Christ.

My prayer is that we would not live in an anti-vision, simply looking for fair punishment in the midst of injustice or being content when punishment is given. My prayer is that we would truly seek reconciliation. You can have justice without reconciliation, but you can't have true reconciliation without justice. Christ was able to reconcile us to God because he dealt with our injustices and sin. There was punishment, and he bore it. In the same way, whenever we are dealing with injustices between one another, we must deal with the injustice, but we must do so with a heart of reconciliation. Our posture must remain humble, allowing God through his Holy Spirit and his family to correct us and redirect us all along the way. Our hearts are inclined to wander and need constant realignment with Christ in order for us to truly see others the way Christ does and pursue reconciliation. This is what it means to be an advocate.

Why Do We Run to the Tension?

Advocates run into the tension, but they don't do so aimlessly. Advocates run to the tension *with a heart toward reconciliation*. Fighting aggravators run into the tension all the time. What distinguishes an advocate is the posture of their heart.

Remember, Onesimus was a runaway slave who was converted to Christianity while in prison with Paul. Paul could have asked him to stay. Paul could have sent him to another church. But instead, Paul wanted to show the power of the gospel. He ran to the heart of the tension and sent Onesimus back to Philemon. But he didn't just run to the tension without any purpose or strategy. He ran to the tension to see reconciliation between Onesimus and Philemon, as brothers.

To "Keep It Real"

A lot of times those who run to the tension are what I like to call the "keep it real people." They say things like, "Okay, I'm just gonna keep it real." They run to the tension and keep it real, but they don't really care whose feelings are hurt. If there's tension and nobody's saying anything about it, then they're happy to get everything out in the open.

But the example Paul set for us is different. He had no desire to be an aggravator, and he wanted to deal lovingly with all parties involved.

To Appease Our Guilt

Others might run to the tension to appease their guilt. They want to feel good about themselves. We see this all the time nowadays. We can try to appease our guilt in any number of ways: by posting about an issue on social media, by reading a couple good books to get woke, by making friends with someone on the other side of the divide.

But attempts to appease our guilt aren't the attempts of a true advocate. If you're just trying to appease your guilt, the only person you're advocating for is . . . yourself. Advocates are altogether different. Advocates run to the tension with purpose: to bring about reconciliation.

To Bring True Reconciliation

In true reconciliation, there are a couple of things always present: acceptance and repentance. Both of these are found in forgiveness, which is absolutely critical in order to bring true reconciliation. When a person forgives someone who did not ask for it, this frees the offend*ed*. On the flip side, when a person genuinely asks for forgiveness but is denied, this frees the offend*er*. So in one case we have acceptance without repentance, and in another we have repentance without acceptance.

The Bible tells us to do all that we can to be at peace with everyone (Rom. 12:18). In order to have true reconciliation, we need both acceptance and repentance. We've got to deal with the real issues of our hearts. Paul is going to challenge Philemon to accept Onesimus while simultaneously calling Onesimus to repentance. The two men will never be reconciled without both of these being present.

We see this illustrated in Matthew 18 when Jesus is talking about disciplining brothers and sisters who have gone wayward. He gives instructions to first go before a person individually, and after that, to bring others along. If there is still no repentance, bring him before the church. And a lot of times we respond to these guidelines just like Peter did. We take it literally and say, "Alright I did all three steps! Am I done now? Can I be done with this?" Peter responds to Jesus and says, "What if I forgive seven times? Now am I justified?"

But what does Jesus say? "No, Peter; you've missed it. It's not seven times. It's seventy times seven. Do *everything* you can to bring about true reconciliation" (see Matt. 18:21–22).

Jesus continues and tells a story of a man who owes a king many lifetimes worth of debt. No matter how much he worked, he would never be able to repay all he owed. The king responds and forgives the man's debt. But then, the forgiven man goes out and finds another slave who owes him a lot of money—but it's not many lifetimes' worth, it's only one lifetime's worth. And instead of offering forgiveness, he has the man thrown into prison.

When the king hears about the forgiven man's unwillingness to forgive his slave, he says, "Why are you, who have been forgiven so much, unwilling to forgive others?" And then the king has him put him back in prison. And Jesus ends the story right there (Matt. 18:21–35).

Our church families are filled with people who are dealing with a lot of grief and pain. We are faced with a lot of issues with people inside the church, outside the church, people who support

President Trump, people who don't support him, and a lot of other things. There's so much pain and so much animosity and so much drama involved in these conflicts. But if we don't deal with it, who's the one who ends up in prison? Who's the one left in bondage? The one unwilling to forgive. The one who won't seek reconciliation. The one who simply aggravates without ever advocating for reconciliation to Christ and to one another.

Not only have we been commanded to be reconciled to one another, we have been given the ministry of reconciliation (2 Cor. 5:18). To do anything less than run to the tension of injustice with a heart toward reconciliation is to miss the call God has placed on our lives.

In 2 Corinthians 5:16–17, Paul starts by telling us that we must learn to see people differently; we can no longer know or see people from a worldly perspective. This means that when we look at believers, we must see them as people who are raised with Christ. And for unbelievers, we must see them as people whom God can raise for the sake of Christ.

But seeing people differently is rooted in how we think God sees us. When we really recognize how Christ now views us differently, how he has saved us and made us his ambassadors and advocates, that realization changes how we view others. We are to see others as new creations or potential new creations! As those who are in Christ, or who might be soon.

This is what frustrates me and grieves me deeply about the way Christians often view themselves and one another. We tend to be more defined by the adjectives in front of what it means to be new creations in Christ than we are defined by the Christ we are in! Labels can be so divisive because they reveal that we see one another primarily through what divides us rather than what unites us.

Now, by no means am I saying that we are to live in a "colorblind society"—we couldn't do that even if we wanted to. And I'm not saying we should ignore our differences or fail to acknowledge where people are or who people are. What I'm saying is that *we are to recognize the one who unites us over the things that divide us.* That is the only way we will ever be able to celebrate unity within diversity.

Doing life and ministry in the Old Fourth Ward, I wrestle with these tensions all the time. You see, in my neighborhood, the tension is thick between the indigenous and the gentrified. They both take pride in who they are. Those who are gentrifying say things like, "If we could only get rid of the Section 8 housing, then our neighborhood would be great." But those who are indigenous to the context see all the new people coming and going, and they take great pride that they have been there the longest, that this is the neighborhood their grandparents lived in, that this is their home turf. The pride on both sides creates this tension.

I tell our church all the time that we are one bad event away from Ferguson happening in our neighborhood. Why? Because of the tension between different groups of people. We see one another as enemies instead of friends. We see one another with a worldly perspective instead of a godly perspective. And that is just my neighborhood! Imagine how differently our neighborhoods around the country might look if Christians saw the "others" with a godly perspective. Whether those "others" are White folks, Black folks, brown folks, immigrants, refugees, rich, poor, English speakers, non-English speakers, politicians, police officers, you name it. Our call in the love of Christ is to view people with a godly perspective, and this is why our church strives to run straight into the tensions of our neighborhood—because we hope to show a picture of what true unity can look like and display that the answer to gentrification is not the relocation of the poor, but the gospel made visible through the local church.[2] But this only happens through a reconciled church that sees people as siblings (or future siblings) instead of enemies, that treats people like people and not obstacles to be overcome.

Imagine the perspective change both Philemon and Onesimus were challenged to take. Philemon, who viewed Onesimus as a slave, an employee, and a runaway rebel. Onesimus, who saw Philemon as the obstacle to his freedom, the man in power who needed to be escaped from. And Paul tells Philemon to receive Onesimus as a *brother*. Can you imagine? Philemon hadn't been the one who led Onesimus to Christ. He didn't have that kind of relational bond with him. He was going off of past experience and looking in the face of a runaway slave. And yet, Paul pleads with him to look at Onesimus altogether differently—to receive him as a brother.

Remember how Joseph responded to his brothers when they came to Egypt during the famine? He (after the initial back and forth) threw them a feast and welcomed them like he welcomed no other travelers. Why? Because they were his brothers. They were family. And that type of dramatic change is exactly what Paul challenges Philemon to do. Look at Onesimus and see a brother.

Advocates Are Needed in Hostile Areas

Before we take a further look at 2 Corinthians 5, I want to show you how closely related the words *advocate* and *ambassador* are. Let's look again at how we defined *advocate* in the beginning of this book.

---

[2] Mark Dever, *The Church: The Gospel Made Visible* (Nashville, TN: B&H Publishing, 2012).

Webster's definition of an *advocate*:
Advocate:

1. one who pleads the cause of another; specif-
    ically: one who pleads the cause of another
    before a tribunal or judicial court
2. one who defends or maintains a cause or
    proposal
3. one who supports or promotes the interests
    of a cause or group[3]

And let's look at the definition of an *ambassador.*
Webster's definition of an *ambassador*:
Ambassador:

1. an official envoy; especially: a diplomatic
    agent of the highest rank accredited to a
    foreign government or sovereign as the
    resident representative of his or her own
    government or sovereign or appointed for
    a special and often temporary assignment
2a. an authorized representative or messenger
2b. an unofficial representative[4]

In so many ways, the functions and identity of an ambassador and an advocate are the same. In a legal sense, obviously an
ambassador has a different type of authority. And I think that is
important to remember, that as ambassadors for Christ, we have
the authority of the King, and we use that authority to advocate
for reconciliation. So, understanding that we are ambassadors

---

[3] https://www.merriam-webster.com/dictionary/advocate
[4] https://www.merriam-webster.com/dictionary/ambassador

for Christ and the authority that lies therein, for the sake of consistency, throughout most of the book I'm going to stick to the term *advocate* as another way to describe our identity and role as ambassadors. But first, I want to take a closer look at how Paul describes our identity as ambassadors.

Let's look at 2 Corinthians 5:20. Paul writes, "Therefore, we are ambassadors for Christ, since God is making his appeal through us. We plead on Christ's behalf: 'Be reconciled to God.'" Paul is reminding us in this verse that our identity drives our activity. Paul wants believers to understand their identity in Christ because it's only when we understand our identity as reconcilers and ambassadors that we begin to act as reconcilers and ambassadors.

God is reconciling the world to himself (2 Cor. 5:19), so as we are in our variety of homes and workplaces and circles of influence, we are also to plead on Christ's behalf because he has given us the ministry of reconciliation. If you just look at 2 Corinthians 5:16–20, you will see that reconciliation is mentioned five times. But Paul is sure to clarify that it starts with our identity. God reconciled us to himself and gave us the ministry of reconciliation, thereby making us ambassadors. This is who we are. We are ambassadors. Therefore, we "plead on Christ's behalf, 'Be reconciled to God.'"

J. B. Lightfoot wrote this about ambassadors: "Ambassadors authoritatively announce messages for others and request, not demand acceptance. The Christian ambassador ('ambassador for Christ'), moreover, announces and appeals for God ('as though God were making an appeal through us')."[5] Any time we engage difficult issues, we get to represent the kingdom of heaven. We

---

[5] J. B. Lightfoot, *Ordination Addresses and Counsels to Clergy* (London and New York: Macmillan, 1891), 47–48.

get a chance to live out our identity as reconcilers and speak on Christ's behalf, to be the very conduits of God's grace of bringing together what sin has divided. This often requires going into hostile territory. Lightfoot explained ambassadors further, writing,

> In the Roman Empire, there were two kinds of provinces, the senatorial and the imperial. The senatorial provinces were generally peaceful and friendly to Rome. They had submitted to Roman rule and were under the control of the Senate. The imperial provinces, however, had been acquired later, and were not as peaceful. These provinces were under the authority of the emperor himself. Syria, including Judea, was such an imperial province. To these provinces, the emperor sent ambassadors to govern and maintain peace."[6]

So according to Lightfoot, the role of an ambassador was primarily the role of going into hostile territory. Ambassadors were most needed, not in peaceful areas, but in hostile areas in order to bring peace.

Advocates experience this same hostility. Advocates are not needed where there is unity—only where there is division. And division, by nature, is most often hostile. When two or more parties are divided and fighting for their positions, it can feel like an absolute war zone. And this is why, perhaps, our final characteristic of an advocate is so important.

---

[6] Ibid.

CHAPTER 5

Advocates Respond with Dignity

One of the ways aggravators often miss the mark in their engagements with racial division is by failing to show dignity. Often, when we disagree with someone, we reduce them to our least favorite aspects about them, rather than seeing them as people made in the image of God. Paul's example corrects us, as the final trait we see him exemplify is responding with dignity.

Advocates Respond with Dignity by Relating to All Parties with Concern

The first way we see this is that Paul responds with dignity by relating to all parties with concern. This doesn't simply mean we should express that we care for all people involved, it also means we express the same level of respected interest in the various opinions present. It's easy to understand points of views that are similar to our own, but most times we don't even try to understand where the other person is coming from.

Many Christians who voted for Clinton or a third party can't imagine why someone would vote for Trump. And many Christians who voted for Trump can't imagine why someone would have voted for Clinton. A lot of times we don't even stop to ask questions about another person's perspective—we just assume the worst. The golden rule tells us to treat others like we want to be treated. So, in any of the issues, no matter where I stand, I would want someone to consider me and my perspective with respect and dignity.

We are never ever going to be able to eliminate our cultural distinctives. And we don't want to. Even at the heavenly worship service, God still recognizes different ethnicities. John didn't see a multitude "who used to be from every nation, tribe, people, and language," but "a vast multitude from every nation, tribe, people, and language" (Rev. 7:9–10). We are always going to have differences, and that's wonderful. God created us different on purpose. But as advocates, we have to be concerned about the unity of our family—unity *in* diversity.

Paul says to Philemon, "I am sending him back to you—I am sending my very own heart" (Philem. 12). He establishes his concern for Onesimus. He already established his concern for the household of Philemon at the beginning of the letter, when he addressed Philemon as his dear brother and co-laborer. Paul expresses care for Philemon's household while simultaneously expressing deep care and concern for Onesimus. For Paul to be able to advocate for unity among these brothers, they each needed to know that he was genuinely concerned for them, and that he respected their situation, viewpoint, and perspective.

Advocates Respond with Humility
Rather than Superiority

Once Paul expresses his concern, he's able to respond with humility rather than superiority. This is another powerful way we respond with dignity toward others. He says in verses 13–14, "I wanted to keep him with me, so that in my imprisonment for the gospel he might serve me in your place. But I didn't want to do anything without your consent, so that your good deed might not be out of obligation, but of your own free will."

What I love about these verses and even about this book is that you see Paul placing himself in the place of an advocate for both parties. At times, it's like Paul sits on Philemon's side and argues to Onesimus on behalf of Philemon. But then at other times, it's like Paul sits on Onesimus's side and argues to Philemon on behalf of Onesimus. As I studied this text and saw Paul's response, I was reminded of the story in Joshua 5:13–14 when the Israelites were about to go in and conquer Jericho.

> When Joshua was near Jericho, he looked up
> and saw a man standing in front of him with a
> drawn sword in his hand. Joshua approached
> him and asked, 'Are you for us or for our ene-
> mies?' 'Neither,' he replied. "I have now come
> as commander of the Lord's army.' Then Joshua
> bowed with his face to the ground in worship.

Paul is not about simply helping someone win the battle. He wants to win the war, and the war, is about having two reconciled brothers—not about proving someone was wrong. Too many of us are more concerned with being right than we are with being reconciled. And right here, the soldier gives us a powerful picture when he responds and tells Joshua he is not for Israel *or* for their adversaries. He is for the Lord.

Paul could have used his position as an apostle to tell Philemon what to do. He could have said, "Listen, Philemon. I'm the Lord's apostle. He appeared to me and called me and commissioned me. He gave me authority, so you better do what I'm telling you to do." But instead, Paul responds differently. He says, "Look, I wanted to keep this brother whom I love, who's dear to me, who's serving me in the midst of my pain." (Remember, Paul's in prison right now.) But in the midst of his pain and bondage, he sends Onesimus back. Paul didn't use his position as an apostle to manipulate Philemon. Rather, he used his identity as a brother to advocate for Onesimus to be reconciled. Paul is demonstrating a humility that reminds us that this life is not all about us. It's not about whether or not your president of choice got elected. God is about his glory. Reconciliation honors the Lord in a way that proving our righteousness never could. To be advocates, we must be willing to take on the most humble positions and the most humble approaches so that we can truly be a part of reconciliation.

Advocates See One Another as Siblings

Another way advocates respond with dignity is by seeing others as brothers and sisters. Verses 15–16 allude to it as Paul writes, "For perhaps this is why he was separated from you for a brief time, so that you might get him back permanently, no longer as a slave, but more than a slave—as a dearly loved brother. He is especially so to me, but how much more to you, both in the flesh and in the Lord."

True forgiveness is not forgetfulness, but true forgiveness is also not servitude. A lot of times we will say, "I'll forgive you but I ain't gonna forget." I see it in spouses all the time. When we make the claim that we aren't going to forget how someone wronged us, we are essentially saying, "Yeah, I'll forgive you, but I'm always going to hold this over your head. I'm always going to allow this to hover over you because I want you to be enslaved to it. I want to keep you in my debt." Paul challenges Philemon—in such a countercultural way—not to receive Onesimus in the same way as before. Receive him instead as a brother. This echoes the same goal we see in Matthew 18:15 where the goal of reconciliation is winning, or gaining, your brother!

Again, if we go to 2 Corinthians 5:16–17, Paul tells us not to see people from a worldly perspective. We must see believers as our brothers and sisters. We must see nonbelievers as potential brothers and sisters. And we must see ourselves humbly, as those who are sinners bought by the blood of Jesus with no place to stand in judgment or superiority over others.

If we really want to overcome the issues of our day, it's not simply about us doing something different. It's really about us seeing one another differently. Until we see one another as brother, sister, co-heirs with Christ, we will continually treat one another with distance. The gospel doesn't make us *like* family, the gospel makes us *family*! That's what Paul is saying. That's the power of the gospel.

God demonstrates his love toward us in that while we were sinners, Christ died for us (Rom. 5:8). In Christ, you and I have been given the most supernatural reconciliation the world has ever known. We were enemies of God and now we are his *children*. But we're not adopted as only children—we're adopted into a family. As his children, we are commissioned and empowered to be supernaturally reconciled to our brothers and sisters.

As we reconcile with one another, we aren't just talking about proximity. We aren't talking about coming to our church service that has this many language groups spoken and then we all leave and don't know anyone else. We are saying we are really family. We are truly one in Christ.

But one of the mistakes we make is in thinking that to be family, we must all think the same things in the same way. It's okay for you to be your own man. Your own woman. We are held together by our common love for Christ. We love him more than we love the Electoral College, more than we love our democracy, more than we love our cultural preferences. In comparison to Christ, they all pale. This is why Jesus says, "If anyone wants to come after me he must hate his father, mother, sister, and brother" (Luke 14:26–28).

We are far too concerned about being "Black enough," "conservative enough," "Reformed enough," "whatever it is enough." We begin to ask the question, *what would my party do?* instead of asking the question, *what would Jesus do?* Being united in Christ does not mean that in the next election everyone is going to vote Democrat, or that everyone's going to vote Republican, or third party. We are always going to be voting in multiple different ways. And please hear me say, *that's okay.* Our identity as the family of Christ outweighs the divisions partisan politics try to create. The gospel tells us that even though you may be different from me, even though you voted differently than I did, even though your opinions are different, even though we disagree on almost everything, I still accept you because you're my brother. You're my sister. We are family.

Advocates Respond with Dignity
by Showing Compassion

Paul says that God calls us to receive one another again—no matter how heinous the crime—seventy times seven times, as brothers, not servants. Because it's in that brotherly reception that we begin to respond with dignity through compassion. In verses 17–22, Paul writes,

> So if you consider me your partner, receive him as you would receive me. If he has wronged you at all, or owes you anything, charge that to my account. I, Paul, write this with my own hand: I will repay it—to say nothing of your owing me even your own self. Yes, brother, I want some benefit from you in the Lord. Refresh my heart in Christ. Confident of your obedience, I write to you, knowing that you will do even more than I say. At the same time, prepare a guest room for me, for I am hoping that through your prayers I will be graciously given to you. (ESV)

In these verses, we see clearly that the goal of the gospel is to restore the dignity of man. Every human is created in the image of God. The problem is that sin and brokenness don't allow us to experience God's original design. But reconciliation allows us to recover and pursue God's original design for us.[1] The gospel reconciles us to God and to one another, and in reconciling those relationships it renews our God-given dignity.

This is why the gospel says to the privileged, "You need to think more lowly of yourself. You aren't God's gift to the earth."

---

[1] http://lifeonmissionbook.com/conversation-guide

But to those who walk around like Eeyore, the gospel says, You need to think more highly of yourself (see James 1:9–10). The reality is that as believers in Christ, we are all peers at the foot of the cross. We were all created in the image of God, we all sinned and fell short of the glory of God, and we have all received an equal inheritance from Christ. In him, there are no rankings. No one is more lowly than another (Gal. 3:26–29). And this is our goal: to make that spiritual reality become a present reality.

We have to reject the notion that people are either greater than me or less than me. Sometimes it's a subtle distinction that comes to light when we honestly assess the way we view those whose opinions do not align with ours. These distinctions are dividing us.

Paul says we are all image bearers with equal dignity, and he says when we see divisions happening, we are not to passively sit back. When we see anyone being treated as less than God's image-bearer, we must speak up as advocates. No matter someone's beliefs or political opinions, it is always sinful to dishonor the dignity that God has bestowed on every human. As advocates, we have the opportunity and responsibility to speak on behalf of those who are being treated without dignity.

Being an advocate and reinforcing dignity does not mean we agree with everyone. We can reinforce someone's dignity and still disagree with their opinions. If we are not able to see a person's dignity in the midst of disagreements, then we will become just like the world.

Modeling the Advocacy of Christ

Paul says, "Let me be clear: If Onesimus does owe you something, I'm going to take it out of my own pocket and pay you.

Don't look to him to pay you back. I'll pay you back. I'll be his advocate." What we see here is that Paul became a type of Christ, modeling the sacrifice of Jesus to advocate for us and reconcile us to the Father.

Jesus reconciled us to God by bearing in himself the punishment that was required for our sins, the sacrifice that could appease God's wrath. Here, Paul does the same thing, on a smaller scale. Rather than sending Onesimus back into a situation where he would be received but would still have a debt hanging over his head, Paul paid that debt for him. He stood in the gap and paid the price to reconcile these two men.

Paul's reflection of the supernatural reconciliation of God is a powerful witness and example for us to follow. Imagine if your entire church family lived that way. What a privilege we get as a family to reflect, however so dimly, the absolute glory of Christ. Just as Christ was our advocate and honored our dignity and loved us in spite of our sin, now we get the opportunity to extend the same supernatural love and grace to our brothers and sisters. And in doing so, I pray the words of Jesus will ring true: "By this everyone will know that you are my disciples, if you love one another" (John 13:35).

PART 3

HOW DO WE GET THERE?

CHAPTER 6

Developing a Strategy

Let's do a quick recap. We've covered a lot of ground so far. We started with awareness, looking at the fact that racial division is a real problem, a problem perpetuated by the fact that most of us are aggravators. Then we explored three different types of aggravators: fighting aggravators, fleeing aggravators, and frozen aggravators. Then we looked at the Scriptures (specifically Philemon) to get a vision for the type of people God is calling us to be, and explored what it means to live as advocates. From Philemon, we saw that advocates rely on Christ, run to the tension, and respond with dignity. That's where God wants us to be, so the question becomes, *how do we get there?* How do we go from being aggravators to becoming advocates?

You may be surprised by how simple it is. Now, I'm not saying it is easy. But I do believe it is very simple. I think the clearest steps to help us become advocates are found in Matthew 7:12–14, otherwise known as the Golden Rule.

> "Therefore, whatever you want others to do
> for you, do also the same for them, for this is
> the Law and the Prophets. Enter through the
> narrow gate. For the gate is wide and the road
> broad that leads to destruction, and there are
> many who go through it. How narrow is the
> gate and difficult the road that leads to life, and
> few find it."

Within these three verses, we're going to look at three basic principles that help us become advocates so we can "REP" Christ well.

Now, I don't normally use acronyms, but it's something we do as preachers to help us outline things in our head. So bear with me. In this passage we see that we need to *reflect personally, empathize corporately, and pursue reconciliation.* These principles allow us to become people who represent (or REP) Christ well, which is exactly what we need to become advocates.

Reflect Personally

Let's start with R: Reflect Personally. You may or may not realize this, but the Golden Rule is a principle that resonates across a lot of different literatures, cultures, and religions.[1] It's like Jesus is starting here with a baseline principle that there is a certain level of dignity that all people should expect to give and to receive. We should treat others the way we want to be treated.

But inherent in these instructions is a call to first have an intimate understanding of how you want to be treated. There's

---

[1] C. S. Lewis argues a similar point in the second lecture of *The Abolition of Man.*

a level of understanding we need to have about ourselves before we can discern how we will treat others. Verse 12 starts with the word "therefore" because Jesus is coming to a conclusion from things said in the previous verses. So let's look back really quickly. Earlier in Matthew 7, Jesus talks about taking the log out of your own eye before removing the speck from your brother's eye. This echoes the same call to reflect on your own life before you cast judgment or decide how to treat someone. Jesus continues this same thread of instruction by saying that you need to reflect on how you would like to be treated.

Reflection is critical because the Golden Rule is qualitative, not quantitative. What I mean is that Jesus isn't talking about how many (quantity) people or "who" you are to treat in a certain way, but he's talking about *how* (quality) you are to treat all people. And the answer is that you treat people with the same dignity, the same respect, the same love, and the same reverence you desire others to have for you. But like most simple principles, this is much easier said than done.

We all have a problem with objectivity when it comes to issues concerning injustice and racial division. The problem we have being objective stems from our hearts, hunches, humanity, history, and heritage. Too many of us, when we hear the latest news headline, we automatically jump to a conclusion before we know the facts or learn any details of the case. We act as if we just "know" what the truth is—and that's coming from our hunches. And where did we get those? For us to even begin to look at an issue with any type of clarity, we have to know what to do with our hunches. If not, then they become like facts to us, and we use them to guide our decisions.

Another problem we all have with objectivity is our humanity. The reality is that our humanity will always limit us from knowing everything. We are not sovereign. We are not omnipresent. So if we are never guaranteed to know the whole story with complete accuracy, then how can we presume to have complete objectivity?

Our history limits our objectivity too. We have to recognize that our past shapes our current perspective. No one comes with pure objectivity into any situation. And it's not just our past experiences that shape that, but our cultural heritage as well. Both the events in our life up to this point (our history) and the cultural background in which those events occurred (heritage) shape how we see the present. Whether we like it or not, our worldviews are influenced by our culture. Our biases are different and can take different forms. Sometimes our bias is based on a lived experience with a person or a system. Sometimes it is based on ideas or stereotypes we've been taught or seen in the media. But no matter which type of bias or where it came from, it will impact the way we view people, systems, and situations moving forward.

And so in light of all of these factors, within the Golden Rule, I think the first thing Jesus is calling us to do is to step back and conduct some personal evaluations. We need to take time to walk through these areas of our lives, identifying how our hearts, hunches, humanity, history, and heritage are playing a role in our viewpoint so that we can better understand that we are not coming from a purely objective standpoint.

Russell Moore, president of the Ethics and Religious Liberty Commission, says this as it relates to how our culture impacts us as we interpret the killings of Black youth by police, specifically: "White Americans tend, in public polling, to view the presenting situations as though they exist in isolation, dealing only with the known facts of the case at hand of whether there is evidence of murder. Black American polls show that they tend to view these crises through a wider lens. The question of whether African American youth are too often profiled and killed in America."[2] What Russell Moore is saying is, "We need to understand that we have a cultural bias that has been shaped through our history and heritage, and it brings about a certain approach to situations. And we need to recognize that." I think this is a very important factor, so I want to share with you a little bit about my hunches, history, humanity, and heritage as I approach this subject matter.

When I hear about another shooting of an unarmed Black man, the first emotion I feel is anger and frustration. When I search YouTube and I type in police brutality, my frustration only grows. But is it because of some objective view that I have to know what's going on in each situation? No, it's based on my history, the experiences I've had, the negative realities of systemic injustice that I have faced. It's based on my past. It's based on my heritage.

You see, I grew up in a very pro-Black family. I grew up in a very political family. I grew up in a family that told me not to trust the White man. And even though we were around people from a lot of different ethnic backgrounds, I grew up with an attitude of, "You've gotta keep one eye open. Don't trust people who aren't your own."

There was this tension that it was okay to be friends with White people as long as you weren't *too* close of friends. And while that was never explicitly said to me, it was all around me, and it began to shape my worldview. But it wasn't only my family environment that shaped my worldview in this way. Every time I stepped out of my house, these realities, or perspectives, were played out and reinforced (at least in my world) to be true.

---

[2] https://www.russellmoore.com/2014/11/24/ferguson-and-the-path-to-peace/

In the formative years of my life, middle and high school, I remember having the annual Black and White fight at our schools. A younger student might ask, "Why are we fighting?" And the response was always, "I don't know, but just go get 'em." We did this *every year* of middle school.

I remember in 1989 a group of Mexican-Americans literally stopping our truck with a bunch of guns and knives. We jumped out. They chased us. I was like, "What's going on?" and one of the other two African Americans said, "Man, I don't know, just get up and run." I didn't know what it was about, but I got up and ran.

I grew up with racial tension surrounding me on every side. All throughout high school I remember division between Blacks, Latinos, and the kind of White heavy-metalers. Racial divisions were fueled by a gang mentality and resulted in regular organized fights.

These stories are part of my history and heritage, and they shaped my heart.

I also remember in the spring of 1993, the racial relations hit a boiling point in our school because of the Rodney King beating. I remember that all too vividly. It was heightened because of the coverage the incident received on national television.

I remember after the OJ trial there was a group of Black people celebrating and a group of White people frustrated.

While these national incidents impacted our community, I had other experiences that hit even closer to home. In the spring of 1994 I got in a car accident with my cousin (who was driving the other car). We got out, looked at the damage, and didn't know what we were supposed to do. But we decided since we were cousins, we should just deal with it when we got back home. So we drove away together. And it wasn't but three blocks later I was pulled over by the cops. Instead of asking us any questions, the cops made us both get out of our cars and sit on the ground with our hands up, treating us both like criminals.

I remember later on in that same year, I was with a group of my cousins and friends going to visit another group of friends in an apartment complex. When we arrived, our friends weren't there, so we immediately left. Just a few blocks down the road, all of a sudden, we were pulled over by cops with a bunch of flashlights and guns pointed at our door. They were all shouting, "Freeze! Put your hands up!" They were yelling at us from all sides of the car. I remember my one cousin was asleep in the car while all of this was going on. They're yelling at us and it's frantic and crazy and they're like, "Get your hands up!" and he's obviously not responding because he's asleep. So we hit him. So he's startled and he jumps. And I literally remember thinking, *Oh, God. They're about to kill us.*

I still remember the time when my wife and I were riding in the car with two other African Americans. We get pulled over by the police for driving four miles over the speed limit. They told all of us to get out of the car and then pulled Angie aside (the only White person) so they could ask her in private, "Have they kidnapped you?" These are only a few of the stories and incidents that are ingrained in my heart and my mind.

So today, when you watch YouTube videos or clips on the news and begin to see all the different scenarios and you hear people say, "That could've been me," it's not an exaggeration. Every single one of those incidents I learn about leads me to think, "That *truly* could've been me. I could've been that one." So when I hear about police brutality, when I hear about any situation of injustice where cops are involved, I don't give cops the benefit of the doubt. Why? Because I remember. Because I remember these stories from my history and it shapes the way I view situations today.

So I recognize that there's a bias in me. I'm not coming objectively to these issues. I can't, because I've been shaped by my past. This happens to the point where my wife and I know that any time I get pulled over, whether I'm with my kids or not, the police will ask me to get out of the car. It happens every single time. And so the first thing that Angie does if I see those blue lights is tap me gently and say, "Dhati, it's okay." Why? Because I remember.

When Jesus tells us to treat others the way we want to be treated, he is calling us to personally reflect and recognize that our hunches, humanity, heart, history, and heritage *are* shaping our current view of reality. What I'm saying is that none of us are viewing any situation in isolation, without some sort of bias tinting our viewpoint. There's a certain way that we view reality and it's shaped by our past. And Jesus says in the golden rule, "Treat others the way you want to be treated." In order for us to really know how to do that, we must reflect, we must come to a better understanding of our own perspective. And when we do this first, it enables us to better fulfill the next aspect of the Golden Rule—empathizing corporately.

Empathize Corporately[3]

Empathy causes us to imaginatively put ourselves into the shoes of others, to understand their perspective, to give dignity to their viewpoint, to allow ourselves to connect with the emotions that motivated their actions. When Jesus tells us to treat

---

[3] Much of the content from Empathize Corporately is adapted with permission from Stephanie Powell's blog, "Empathy: A Bridge for Racial Reconciliation," http://betheblueprint.net/2018/02/07/empathy-a-bridge/.

others the way we want to be treated, there are two qualitative things we have to understand. First, we have to recognize we don't live life in a vacuum. Our life experiences shape the way we perceive others (reflect personally). But then the second part is that it is also our responsibility to put ourselves in the shoes of the "other," to take on their views. As I think about the obstacles that keep us from empathizing corporately, two things come to mind. One, we have objectified (or dehumanized) people who are different from us or who hold different views. And two, we have become desensitized to the issues we are dealing with. Both of these issues can be tied to a root problem of not dealing with our emotions.

Our society teaches us many lies about our emotions. We try to hide them, suppress them, or cover them up in fear of being perceived as weak or "too emotional." But emotions are a gift from the Lord and a critical component of reconciliation. Our emotions are the tools that empower us to become skilled empathizers in order to fuel deep connections in the midst of racial (and other) differences.

Emotions are not ultimate—and we will talk more later about being present in our emotions while also submitting them to Christ. But for now, I want to spend some time exploring more about why we need our emotions in pursuit of reconciliation.

Dr. Brenè Brown is a researcher and storyteller who has spent more than sixteen years studying shame, empathy, vulnerability, and courage.[4] Her findings in this area have been foundational to my personal understanding of the role empathy plays in racial reconciliation. One key truth she discovered in her research is that empathy fuels connection between people as it connects

---

[4] https://brenebrown.com/

the emotions of one person to another. Empathy, she explains, is based on emotional connection, not experiential similarities.[5]

Practically speaking, because of the country we live in, people of different skin tones have different life experiences.[6] If we cannot empathize with people we don't share experiences with, then our chances for connection decrease dramatically—*especially* when it comes to matters of race.

But thankfully, experience is not what drives empathy.

Maybe some of you reading this book can relate to my experiences with the police or with race-related gang fights. But there's a good chance many of you cannot. You may have never had a negative encounter with the police. Maybe you've never had a gun pointed at you and your friends in a car. You've never experienced an officer assuming you kidnapped your wife because she was a White woman riding with three Black men.

But you do know what it's like to be afraid. You know what it's like to feel angry when you're being falsely accused and not heard. I bet you know what it's like to have someone assume the worst about you, and to be sad, angry, lonely, and ashamed.

All of us share these emotions, and connecting through our shared *emotion*, not mutual experiences, drives empathy.

Brown says that to choose empathy and connect with others, "I have to connect with something in myself that knows that feeling."[7] This means that, as inconvenient as it may be, the

---

[5]   https://www.thersa.org/discover/videos/rsa-shorts/2013/12/Brene -Brown-on-Empathy

[6]   Michael O. Emerson and Christian Smith, *Divided by Faith: Evangelical Religion and the Problem of Race in America* (New York: Oxford University Press, 2000), 7, 17.

[7]   https://www.thersa.org/discover/videos/rsa-shorts/2013/12/Brene -Brown-on-Empathy

only way to become good at empathizing with others is to first become more familiar with your own emotions.

Empathy is an especially hard choice in emotionally charged conversations about racial division. It means that when I respond in a particular way to the shooting of a Black man by a White police officer, you choose to connect with the anger and hurt that I feel. It means that when you share with me the reasons you support a political candidate, I choose to listen to you fully, without cutting you off or assuming the worst about you.

Empathy means we first seek to connect with each other's hearts *without* trying to change anything. This is incredibly challenging because we have so many problems and disagree passionately about how to fix them. The damage done by racism in our country created so much brokenness, so many damaged systems, wounded families, and untold stories. And all of this needs to be addressed.

Extending empathy does *not* mean we can't challenge one another, and it most certainly doesn't mean that we stay silent in the face of injustice. But in the REP model, there is a reason empathizing corporately comes before the pursuit of reconciliation. Empathy is not the only step, but in order for our relational connections to be strong enough to withstand the challenges of pursuing reconciliation together, empathy *must* come before the pursuit of reconciliation. Empathy will build the connections and bridges we need to withstand the challenges of pursuing reconciliation.

And this is where the importance of *corporate* empathy comes in. Empathy is communal by nature; you cannot do it alone. I can't empathize with myself. For empathy to work, there has to be at least two people involved.

In the context of the local church, empathy needs to occur throughout the family, individuals with other individuals, and groups with other groups. Reconciliation is not the ministry God gave to just a few individual Christians; he gave this ministry to his family—to the whole church. All Christians have been reconciled to God, and therefore, we are all given the ministry of reconciliation. This means that we must pursue reconciliation together, as a unified family. Where Satan will use our differences and divisions to keep us apart, empathy, through the power of the Holy Spirit, can create the bridges needed to unify so that the local church can move toward reconciliation (both individually and corporately, in relationships and systems). If we don't do corporate empathy well, we won't be able to pursue reconciliation as a family.

Pursue Reconciliation

So far, we've looked at a lot of different aspects of pursuing reconciliation. But I think the Golden Rule gives us some good handlebars for *how* we pursue reconciliation, or rather, how we become people who pursue reconciliation. This principle is less explicitly stated in the text, so let me share why I see it as the final component of the Golden Rule.

The last few verses of the Golden Rule say this, "Enter through the narrow gate. For the gate is wide and the road broad that leads to destruction, and there are many who go through it. How narrow is the gate and difficult the road that leads to life, and few find it" (Matt. 7:13–14).

In this whole passage, the whole Sermon on the Mount, Jesus has been talking to a group of people corporately. We don't always pick this up reading in English, because the word "you" looks singular to us. In the original language, however, it's a plural "you." "You all are the salt of the earth; you all are the light of the world." Jesus isn't talking to individuals, but talking to us corporately as those who are blessed by being poor in spirit, those who love mercy, those who have been persecuted for righteousness' sake.

And so to this *group* of people, he is saying, "Enter through the narrow gate." This idea of a narrow gate is not simply a way of life—it is everything Jesus has said up to this point in the sermon, but it's more. The gate is Jesus (John 10:9). So what is Jesus saying? "Enter life through *me*." And within this simple statement I see a bold call to put on the mind of Christ.

But what should immediately come to your mind as you hear that call is this: You are incapable of putting on the mind of Jesus by yourself. You are too shaped by your heart, history, and heritage. And this is where the beauty of the *ekklesia*, the church, is on display. God is reconciling a people to himself and to one another. We don't have to do this alone. Jesus says there's a group of people who will take the wide road. But there's a group of people, God's Church, who will walk the narrow road together.

Together, we are new creations in Christ. His Holy Spirit empowers us to put on the mind of Christ, and God gives us a family to support one another, to help us identify our blind spots, to give us space for confession and repentance and reconciliation. The church ought to be the safest place for people to wrestle and struggle. We have the power of Christ and an incredible opportunity to put the reconciling power of the gospel on display.

So we are called to put on Christ in pursuing reconciliation in community, but we often hit a roadblock in this pursuit. There's a lot of controversy in the role that justice plays. Specifically, we run into two roadblocks: one says racial reconciliation is a "social issue" and a "distraction," and tries to avoid and/or prevent any efforts on the part of Christians toward racial reconciliation. Others seek to make social justice ultimate. Both of these attitudes are wrong.

"Racial Reconciliation Is a Social Issue and a Distraction"

Some argue racial justice is a "social issue," and is therefore a distraction for the church. They say things like, "We just need to preach the gospel," but what they fail to realize is that there's no such thing as preaching the gospel in a vacuum. The gospel is always preached in a particular social setting, and when we preach the gospel in a context that includes racial injustice, we must *apply* the gospel to that issue—to fail to do so is to fail to faithfully preach the gospel.

In Micah 6:8, God clearly commands us to act justly; the command is listed right alongside other "gospel" or "spiritual" activities. God does not put acting justly into a separate category, but into a list of what he requires for those who are walking the narrow path. So we simply cannot conclude that justice is merely a social issue and not a spiritual issue. And since the Great Commission commands us not merely to preach and baptize, but also to make disciples by "teaching them to obey everything I have commanded you," to fail to apply the gospel to all of life is to be disobedient to the Great Commission.

"Social Justice Is Ultimate"

At the same time, there is another roadblock—the idea that social justice is ultimate. We must recognize that this is not the case. Hear me out as I explain.

God has placed us here as advocates to seek justice by acting justly both as individuals and corporately. While we recognize our responsibility to act justly, we must also remember that final justice will ultimately come from the hand of God. Reconciliation is the call of the Christian. Reconciliation is the call of the advocate.

Did you know it's possible to have justice without reconciliation? You know what that's called? Hell. Without reconciliation, justice is hell. And that's why "the goal of our instruction is love that comes from a pure heart, a good conscience, and a sincere faith" (1 Tim. 1:5). Jesus has "reconciled the world to himself and he has given us the ministry of reconciliation" (2 Cor. 5:18). He's telling us that justice isn't enough. You can have justice without reconciliation. But you can't have reconciliation without true justice.

We can't put acting justly on the side as if it were not a critical component to our spiritual walk with God—both as individuals and as local churches. But at the same time, we must remember that our goal, our aim, and the ministry we've been given is that of reconciliation. Justice alone isn't enough.

The Narrow Path

We serve a God who desires to reconcile a people to himself who haven't been acting justly. Aren't you glad that God doesn't reserve reconciliation to those who act justly?

And I know sometimes we can get in the bad habit of categorizing sins and thinking that some are worse than others. But that is what the whole Sermon on the Mount is about. "You have heard that it was said to our ancestors, do not murder . . . but I tell you, everyone who is angry with his brother or sister will be subject to judgment" (Matt. 5:21–22). Who reading this is guilty of murder?

When we hold our hearts up to God's standard, we all fall dramatically short (Rom. 3:23). And that's the beauty of the gospel. God reconciles even the worst of sinners. So when we engage as advocates, we must come in with an awareness of our own story, our own sin, and our own bias. We must be willing to empathize corporately so that we can pursue reconciliation together.

But Jesus doesn't only talk about the gate in this text. There's a gate—but there's also a road. It's not enough just to say that we are in Christ, or to put on the mind of Christ as if it were a stationary activity or some kind of helmet we simply wear on our heads. We don't enter through the gate and sit down on its other side for the rest of our lives. There's a road to walk; we must *follow* his way.

So think back to my story. It's not enough for me to just all of a sudden be at peace with cops. It's not enough to just work toward the day when Angie no longer has to say, "Dhati, it's okay." That's not the goal. Not for the Christian. In order to act justly and pursue reconciliation, I have to pursue reconciliation with White police officers.

Several years ago one of our White, male church members worked as a police officer. And when he was coming off a shift or about to go on duty, he would come to church dressed in his uniform. And I had to approach him to talk to him because it stirred up all these things in my heart. I had to pursue him and say, "Man, listen. I've got all types of beef with you. I've got all types of bitterness. I know it's not you, but when you put on that uniform, it just does something to me." And we had those conversations and honest dialogues. I need to have many more, but those conversations opened up doors for the Lord to start a new work in my heart. It's in these kinds of vulnerable environments where we really have the opportunity to put on the mind of Christ and walk as he walked. We have the opportunity to act justly and pursue reconciliation, not for the goal of just being right, but for the goal of being reconciled. Reconciled to God and to one another.

This is my prayer for my local church. And this is my prayer for you and your church family as you read this book. I pray that you would be empowered through the power of the Holy Spirit to become advocates by reflecting personally, empathizing corporately, and pursuing reconciliation.[8]

---

[8] See appendix for Practical Strategic Initiatives for using the REP model.

PART 4

WHAT FEARS OR OBSTACLES WILL WE FACE?

CHAPTER 7

Courage

So far we've walked through awareness, vision, and strategy. Our final step is to explore courage by looking at what fears or obstacles we will face that might prevent us from becoming the type of people (advocates) that God desires for us.

This part of the book is tricky because every person can have different fears and different obstacles in their journey to becoming advocates. So, for this section to truly be effective, it will require you take some time apart from reading the book in order to reflect on your own obstacles and the obstacles that are unique to your community. If you don't take time to identify those stumbling blocks, then they will prevent you from truly becoming a community of advocates. Naming these fears and obstacles within your church family will allow you to pray for one another with greater clarity, and support one another better as you walk this journey together.

Four Obstacles

That being said, over the course of the last few years, I have noticed four main obstacles within my own church family. I'm not sure I've had an honest conversation with anyone who hasn't expressed, in some way, that these four have been challenges in their journey. So I'm going to take some time to address those here.

Fragility and Fatigue

The first two obstacles I want to address are fragility and fatigue. While these two are very different, I combined them here because most often people struggle with one or the other, not both. Let's start by looking at fragility.

At the risk of overgeneralizing, I'm going to talk about fragility specifically as a problem for White brothers and sisters—"White fragility"—because, in my experience, White Americans are the only ones who really struggle with this obstacle. That is not to say that those of other races could never have this issue, but only that in my experience, it has been limited to White people.

Robin DiAngelo, a White woman writing for the International Journal of Critical Pedagogy, defines White fragility as "a state in which even a minimum amount of racial stress becomes intolerable, triggering a range of defensive moves. These moves include the outward display of emotions such as anger, fear, and guilt, and behaviors such as argumentation, silence, and leaving the stress-inducing situation."[1] Read that

---

[1] Robin DiAngelo, *International Journal of Critical Pedagogy*, Vol. 3 (3) (2011), 54–70, https://libjournal.uncg.edu/ijcp/article/viewFile/249/116.

definition again. Does it sound familiar? Have you seen it in those around you? In yourself?

When we looked at the fleeing aggravator, we discussed how the response of fragility is a lot like someone whose muscles are out of shape so they don't have the stamina to withstand stress. On the other hand, a fighting aggravator might express his or her fragility by blowing up in anger in response to even a hint of an accusation of prejudice or racism. Why is this the case? Why do so many White Americans, and particularly White Evangelical Christians, struggle with fragility?

There have been entire books written that help to explain different components of why fragility is so prevalent among White people today, so we won't go too far in depth into how we got to this place, but I'd like to try to explain it as simply as I can. Regardless of how we got here, the fact of the matter is that in general, White people in the United States (and particularly communities where the majority of people are White, like many evangelical churches) do not have nearly the same amount of critical conversations or engagement with racial issues as those of other races. For starters, a lot of times engagement happens within minority communities because of the experience of racism. Because most White people do not experience racism on a regular basis, they wouldn't often come home talking about it. Since it's not a part of their regular experience, it's not a part of their regular conversation. And on top of that, whether it be from thinking that colorblindness is the best way to bring racial reconciliation,[2] or because of some of the unseen privileges that

---

[2] George Yancey, *Beyond Racial Gridlock: Embracing Mutual Responsibility* (Downers Grove, IL: InterVarsity Press, 2006).

come with being a part of the majority culture,[3] race conversations and engagement occur substantially *less* often in White homes and communities than they do in those of other racial groups in America.

Even if you disagree with some of what I've said about potential reasons *why* racial engagement occurs less among White communities and families, I do think we can all agree that the conversations and engagement happen less frequently. And this is one of the main causes of White fragility.

A White woman in my church who is married to a Black man shared with me some of her experiences marrying a Black man and what it was like to be around his family (especially toward the beginning of their relationship and marriage). One of the first things she noted was that she initially felt like they talked about race issues *all* the time. She said that her family had probably had fewer than ten conversations in her whole life about ethnic matters and racism, but every single time she was with her husband's family, the issue would come up! She shared that this was one of the biggest adjustments for her because she wasn't used to having those types of conversations on a regular basis.

But White fragility isn't simply a response from a lack of knowledge about how to engage the conversations and issues. Yes, there is fragility in the sense that those "muscles" are out of shape, but there is also fragility that is expressed in quickly triggered defensiveness. In DiAngelo's definition of White fragility, she explains that stress from racial (or ethnic) conversations

---

[3] Peggy McIntosh, *White Privilege: Unpacking the Invisible Knapsack*, https://nationalseedproject.org/images/documents/Knapsack_plus_Notes -Peggy_McIntosh.pdf.

triggers "a range of defensive moves."[4] If you aren't sure if fragility is something you struggle with, a quick way to assess yourself is to think back over the last few times you've engaged in issues of ethnic division and racism. Were you quick to get defensive? Did you feel your blood pressure rising? Did you have the urge to speak before listening? That is probably the easiest way to identify someone who is struggling with fragility.

As local churches, we need to understand that we will have people in our congregations who struggle with fragility. And that is okay. Sometimes when people speak of White fragility, those who live with that reality feel condemned, as if it is the unpardonable sin. I want you to know if you're reading this, that is *not* the case. Our churches ought to be a safe place for you to struggle and a safe place for you to work out these new muscles as you begin to engage these issues more deeply.

The second side of the fragility coin is fatigue. This fatigue is the kind that comes from being worn out and exhausted after years of engaging and not feeling like any change is taking place. As we talked about when we explored the different types of aggravators, fatigue could manifest in passivity, apathy, depressed resignation, or a range of other expressions.

Now, let me be clear, advocates will get tired. We are all humans here and as we engage any difficult issue we are bound to feel fatigue. But when we allow our fatigue to control our responses or to keep us from extending empathy toward others, fatigue becomes a great obstacle to us becoming advocates.

I recently had the opportunity to sit down with a dear pastor, mentor, and friend, Dr. Crawford Loritts. I asked him his thoughts on the exhaustion that comes from engaging in issues

---

[4] DiAngelo, *International Journal of Critical Pedagogy*, 54, https://lib-journal.uncg.edu/ijcp/article/viewFile/249/116.

of racial division and leading a church that is predominantly a different race than he is. (Dr. Loritts is African American and the church he pastors is predominantly White.) He said,

> I remember particularly during the decade of
> my twenties and early thirties, I just got worn
> out. Worn out, you know, because you're in
> no-man's land. On one hand, your own people,
> African Americans, are saying, particularly
> during the seventies, "Why are you with these
> White folks? You're selling out." My ethnic
> authenticity was called into question. And on
> the other hand, White folks that you're working
> with, they didn't quite get it either. Black folks
> say, "So why are you there?" And the White
> folks that you're with say, "Now, why are you
> here?" All of that was important on my journey
> because all of that drove me to a point where I
> had to value obedience and calling over strategy
> and affirmation. And that's what you come back
> to. And so I say this . . . the thing that will keep
> you from losing your mind, from burning out,
> is a realization that God has His hand on you
> to do this. I think a lot of guys get burned out
> because we're looking for something that they
> can't give us.[5]

In the interview, Dr. Loritts was specifically speaking to encourage pastors in multi-ethnic environments, but I think the principle holds true for anyone desiring to be an advocate. If

---

[5] http://betheblueprint.net/2018/05/11/race-2-the-sbc-dr-walter-strickland/

we hope to find restoration and joy and rest from our fatigue in results or the responses of others, we will find ourselves perpetually burned out. But if we understand what the Lord is calling us to do and we run toward him, for him, and rest in him, our fatigue will no longer be able to control us and keep us from responding empathetically or pursuing reconciliation.

No matter if you struggle with fragility or fatigue, we have the ability within the church to love one another in our struggle—to validate the struggles we are each facing, to encourage one another, and to bring dignity to the fragility or fatigue facing those within our church families. But it starts with confession. It starts with a willingness to confess how we are struggling, what our needs are, and praying together for God to give us courage and wisdom to overcome the obstacles in front of us so that we can become the people he intends for us to be.

Misplaced Identity

The next key obstacle I have seen that prevents people from becoming advocates is misplaced identity. When we are adopted into Christ's family, we are given new identities. "The old has passed away, and see, the new has come!" (2 Cor. 5:17). The things that used to *define* us should now only *describe* us. Let me explain what I mean.

Before coming to Christ, I was defined by my abilities as a football player and by being Black. Those two aspects of my life shaped my decisions about college, career, friendships, girlfriends, music, media, and every other aspect of my life. But when I came to Christ, I was given a new identity. And while it has taken a lifelong journey of walking with Christ for some of those other identities to surrender their place to Christ, those things that once defined me now only describe me.

Yes, I am still Black. And yes, my Blackness matters to me, and it matters to God, and there is no need for us to ignore it and the role it has played and continues to play in my life. In fact, as we saw earlier, I'll still be Black in the new creation, when a multitude from every tribe, tongue, and nation is worshiping God.

However, my Blackness does not *define* me. It simply describes one aspect of my life. In the same way, being a football player no longer defines me. It describes something I used to do, teams I used to be a part of, but it does not define who I am, what my purpose is, or guide how I make decisions.

For some reason, it seems to me that Christians really, really like to take on descriptors (which, in and of themselves are not a bad thing) and use them as their identity. Reformed Christian. Arminian Christian. Conservative Christian. Liberal Christian. White Christian. Black Christian. Mega Church. House Church. Attractional Church. Missional Church. Small Group Church. Contemporary Church. Traditional Church. The way we use these labels to define us reminds me a lot of how the Christians in Corinth were using labels to define themselves, too. Look at what Paul had to say to them in 1 Corinthians 1:10–13:

> Now I urge you, brothers and sisters, in the
> name of our Lord Jesus Christ, that all of you
> agree in what you say, that there be no divisions
> among you, and that you be united with the
> same understanding and the same conviction.
> For it has been reported to me about you, my
> brothers and sisters, by members of Chloe's
> people, that there is rivalry among you. What
> I am saying is this: One of you says, "I belong
> to Paul," or "I belong to Apollos," or "I belong
> to Cephas," or "I belong to Christ." Is Christ

divided? Was Paul crucified for you? Or were
you baptized in Paul's name?

Did you catch that? Paul even told them that those who said
"I belong to Christ" were in the wrong! How can that be? They
were being divisive. And God has no room for division within
his family. Notice, Paul didn't say "I urge you that there be no
differences among you," but "that there be no *divisions* among
you." Of course, we will always have differences. Our culture and
background and race and personalities are not erased when we
become Christians. But those differences should not divide us.

I truly believe that a lot of our division comes from misplaced
identities. Again, I do not believe that our differences should be
ignored, overlooked, or taken for granted. I think they should be
displayed and discussed and celebrated. But they should be done
as things that *describe* us, all the while recognizing our common
identity in Christ as what *defines* us.

Christ desires to have preeminence in our life. He's not asking to be first in a list of many. He's asking to be central, the
one and only. Think about it this way. If I go to my wife and say,
"Angie, you know you're my number one girl. But you know I
also got my number two and three girls on the side." Would anyone consider me a faithful husband? No! My posture toward my
wife ought to be, "Angie, you are the *only* woman in my life and I
love and respect you enough to place disciplines and boundaries
in my life so that my fidelity toward you is *never* compromised."
God is after our whole hearts. Every single part of them. This is
the good work he started in us, to conform us to the likeness of
Christ (Rom. 8:29). And for us to become advocates, we must do
the hard work of facing anything that defines us that is divisive
and not of Christ and be willing to surrender that in place of

our identity as children of God and brothers and sisters to one another.

Emotions

The final major hurdle I see toward us becoming advocates is our emotions. I've said it before, but I want to say it again. Emotions are not bad. They are not a sign of weakness. They are not sinful. And like I talked about in the REP section, understanding our emotions is key for us to be able to empathize with others.

So, if emotions aren't bad, why are they an obstacle? Great question. I've listed them as an obstacle because often times, particularly when it comes to dealing with ethnic divisions, we don't deal with our emotions in a healthy way. And so what ends up happening is that our emotions control our responses. When we use emotions as a guide, we act more like aggravators than advocates, because that's not what our emotions are intended to do. Think about it in terms of your car. On your dashboard there are several gauges. One tells you how much fuel you have, another tells you how fast you are going, and another tells you if your car is overheated. These tools are meant to tell you how your car is doing. They are not a GPS. They do not tell you where to go. And the same is true for your emotions. They are your dashboard. They tell you *how* you are doing. They let you know *where* you are—which is a powerful tool to enable you to connect with God and others. But God did not give us emotions to be our GPS or to guide our decision-making. He gave us his Word, his Spirit, and his church for that.

Here's another example. Has anyone ever taught you the valuable lifelong lesson, don't go grocery shopping when you're hungry? Why don't we want to go to the grocery store hungry?

Because we know that when we are hungry, we have a propensity to make decisions that go outside of the boundaries of our grocery list and our budget. So being aware of how hungry you are before you walk into the store can help you stick to your boundaries and make decisions based on your values, not your stomach. Emotional awareness is important for the same reasons. We need to know where we are, how we are feeling, and what propensities we have when we feel certain emotions. I need to know that seeing blue sirens triggers fear in me, and that when I get really afraid I have a propensity to rage out or become disrespectful. Being aware of my emotions and the ways my flesh wants to respond out of them gives me the opportunity to surrender to the Lord, tell him my emotions, and let him instruct the ways I should respond.

Race issues trigger emotions in all of us. They may vary from apathy to rage or fear to deep sorrow. Regardless of what they are for you specifically, if we do not put in the emotional work required to be aware of our hearts and to not allow our emotions to make our decisions for us, then our emotions will continue to drive the way we engage in racial divisions. Instead, we should allow the Holy Spirit to direct our conversations and engagement.

A Final Word of Encouragement

Perhaps the greatest obstacle we will face in our efforts to become godly advocates is the fact that we have an enemy who is actively working to keep us divided. He wants to give us every reason in the world to stay bitter, to stay resentful, to stay arrogant, to act out of justified anger, and to live as aggravators. So I want to look quickly at a couple of different passages of Scripture that I believe help us have courage and hope to continue to fight for unity and reconciliation. First, let's look at a conversation Jesus has with his disciples in Matthew 16:13–19.

> When Jesus came to the region of Caesarea
> Philippi, he asked his disciples, "Who do people
> say that the Son of Man is?" They replied,
> "Some say John the Baptist; others, Elijah;
> still others, Jeremiah or one of the prophets."
> "But you," he asked them, "who do you say
> that I am?" Simon Peter answered, "You are
> the Messiah, the Son of the living God." Jesus
> responded, "Blessed are you, Simon son of
> Jonah, because flesh and blood did not reveal
> this to you, but my Father in heaven. And I also
> say to you that you are Peter, and on this rock
> I will build my church, and the gates of Hades
> will not overpower it. I will give you the keys
> of the kingdom of heaven, and whatever you
> bind on earth will have been bound in heaven,
> and whatever you loose on earth will have been
> loosed in heaven."

What I love about this passage is that Jesus uses wartime language. Think about it. What are gates for? They are used for defensive purposes to keep out the enemy. And Jesus is telling us that the gates of hell will not withstand the attack of his church! This is hope for us. This gives us courage. Christ has already won the battle. He promises that the church will be victorious as we storm the gates of hell. We can move toward unity, pressing deep into the dark and messy spaces of division with full confidence that Jesus will be victorious. Christ's promise of victory is something we can hold onto because it reminds us that our labor is not in vain, our work will not be wasted, and the darkness will not overcome the light. This is *promised* to us!

And even more than promised victory, we are promised the presence of God himself at every single step of our journey. Remember Jesus' final words to his disciples before the ascension? He said, "And lo, I am with you always, even unto the end of the world" (Matt. 28:20 KJV). The presence of God is our provision to become the people he has called us to become. He himself is doing this work in us! When we look at John 15, Jesus is telling his disciples over and over and over again, "Abide in me. Remain in me. Abide in me. Remain in me." He is the vine. He provides all that we need for life and godliness (2 Pet. 1:3). He promises to finish the work he began in us (Phil. 1:6). And what is that work? To conform us into the likeness of his Son (Rom. 8:29). A Son who is our advocate is conforming us to become like himself.

Corrie ten Boom was a Dutch woman living during the Holocaust. Her family was Christian and worked to hide Jews from the Nazis. She was put into a concentration camp and survived to tell her story. After the war ended and the Nazis were no longer in power, she was, at times, forced to come face-to-face with the Nazi soldiers who killed her family in the concentration camp. Few of us have ever had to have courage like that! In the midst of one of these encounters, here's what she wrote.

> Even as the angry vengeful thoughts boiled through me, I saw the sin of them. Jesus Christ had died for this man; was I going to ask for more? *Lord Jesus*, I prayed, *forgive me and help me to forgive him. . . . Jesus, I cannot forgive him. Give me Your forgiveness. . . .* And so I discovered that it is not on our forgiveness any more

than on our goodness that the world's healing
hinges, but on His. When He tells us to love
our enemies, He gives along with the command,
the love itself.[6]

Brothers and sisters, God will give us what we need to
become the advocates he called us to be through the power of the
Holy Spirit living within us and working through us. So as you
go, as you engage, as you succeed, as you fail, as the sins of your
heart are exposed, as God uses your strengths, and as you rely
on him in your weakness, know that you go with the presence
of Almighty God dwelling within you. Know that the work he
began in you, he promises to complete (Phil. 1:6). Abide in him.
Stay close to him, knowing that he will use his church to shine
a light into the darkness, and the darkness will not overcome it
(John 1:5).

---

[6] Corrie ten Boom, Elizabeth Sherrill, and John Sherrill, *The Hiding
Place* (1971; repr., Grand Rapids, MI: Chosen Books, 2006), 247–48.

My little children, I am writing you these things so that you may not sin. But if anyone does sin, we have an advocate with the Father—Jesus Christ the righteous one. He himself is the atoning sacrifice for our sins, and not only for ours, but also for those of the whole world.

1 John 2:1–2

Practical Strategic Initiatives

The REP model tells us how we become advocates, but it does so based on principle—which is helpful, because it can be applied in any context. I want to share with you some of the practical things we've done at our church both to teach REP but also to help our members take their next step toward becoming advocates.

I am not sharing these things so you can copy-and-paste them into your church. I recognize that every context is different, has different needs, and will respond differently to all of these things. But I wanted to share so that you could begin to see some practical ways to help your whole church move toward becoming advocates and begin to dream about what God might have you do in your context.

One of the first ways our leadership decided to respond to some of the racial divisions was to call a community forum or a "race talk." Our church doesn't have a traditional Sunday school hour, but when we feel there's a need, we utilize the hour or so before service to create a more intimate environment for teaching or discussion. One of the first community forums we held was after the Trayvon Martin shooting. The shooting caused a lot of turmoil within our family, and we felt like we needed to address it. So we invited our church to join us for four-to-six weeks on Sunday mornings, and our leaders facilitated conversations among the community. Some weeks we would have different leaders in the community share, or we would have our elders share with the group. Other weeks we would hear from different members of the church and give space for them to share their stories and emotions. We have also facilitated group work where we pair people together to share stories, emotions, and process situations together. We know as leaders that our people are going to be talking about these issues, so we feel it's important to create safe spaces to talk together so that we can hear one another, listen well, and start conversations facilitated by trusted leaders who can lead people toward unity in the midst of different opinions.

During one of our community forum series, we began to realize the role that emotions were playing in how our church was able to engage well in the midst of racial divisions. We also quickly realized that most of our church (and we really think most people in our culture) have an unhealthy understanding of what emotions are and don't know how to use them fully as God intended. And we recognized that not knowing how to engage your own emotions is a major obstacle to empathy and engaging with others in divisive spaces. So we followed up by doing an eight-week sermon series on emotions based on the content learned from Chip Dodd and his work, particularly in the book, *The Voice of the Heart*.[1] The series didn't tie into anything having

---

[1] http://chipdodd.com/books/

to do with racial divisions, but we just really took time to teach on emotions, their value, and their role, and then we used our weekly Missional Community Bible Studies to create space for our church to have more intimate conversations and practice healthy emotional engagement.

Our emotions series happened to fall in a month where we were doing Wednesday night classes at the church. (We do them periodically over a few months in the year.) One of the classes we offered in this series was called "Race and Emotions." In this class we walked people through the REP model, taking one point per week and facilitating group work to help people deal with their emotions as it specifically relates to issues of race and racial divisions. Where the emotions series was focused generally on emotions, this class allowed us to walk more closely with people and create safe spaces to deal with our emotions in regard specifically to issues of racial division. We asked people to write out stories, reflecting on their own experiences relating to their race. Then we asked people to share their stories with one another and respond with empathy, connecting to the emotions in one another's stories and learning how to put themselves in the shoes of others. We worked hard to encourage the class to listen in order to understand instead of listening to respond.

Another way we engaged our congregation with this issue was by preaching through the book of 1 Corinthians in a sermon series called "Reconciled." Problems of division, and particularly racial division, are woven throughout the New Testament. These issues are not new to the church. God's Word has so much to say to them, so we intentionally preached through a book of the Bible that really deals with them. We want our church to know the biblical foundations for the principles we are asking them to live out in their daily lives as it relates to pursuing reconciliation, and our elders felt like preaching through 1 Corinthians would best speak to the needs of our congregation.

All of these things I've listed are short-term, or start-and-stops, as we like to call them. They are not ongoing. They have a start date and an end date, and that allows us to really make sure we are speaking to where our church is in a timely manner. Some of these are planned out months in advance, but other times, we've paused sermon series or called for community forums last minute in response to a real-time event.

These are just a few of the strategic initiatives that our leadership has used to help our church move toward being advocates. Again, please don't see these as constrictive or try to copy them exactly for your context. Use the REP model however it needs to be used to best pursue reconciliation in your community.

How do we turn
PASSIVE PARTICIPANTS
into
ACTIVE DISCIPLE MAKERS
in an ever changing urban context

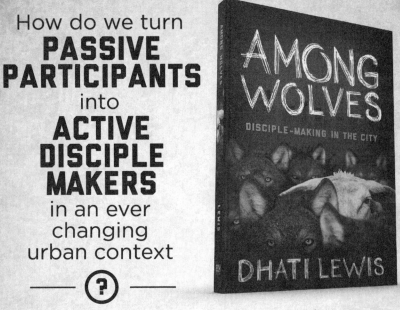

We have reduced Christianity to concerts, conferences, and church services. We are surrounded by passive participants of Christianity, content to soak in information without any intent to make disciples. But the question remains: how do we turn passive participants into active disciple makers in an ever changing urban context?

Among Wolves seeks to help us move to obedience to the call of Christ to labor among wolves. You will walk through eight significant movements in the book of Matthew, beginning with Jesus establishing His presence with us, to Him mobilizing an army to go and make disciples of all nations. As we follow Jesus' patterns and teachings in Matthew, you will be equipped to establish a thriving disciple making culture in your context as your burden to see your city reached moves toward reality.

B&H
PUBLISHING

"

"The Bible translation I use is crucial in preaching and discipleship, because I need *something I can trust and something my people can understand.* The Christian Standard Bible strikes that perfect balance."

DHATI LEWIS